HORNUNG'S HANDBOOK OF
DESIGNS & DEVICES

1836 basic designs and their variations
by one of America's foremost industrial and graphic designers

DOVER PUBLICATIONS, INC., NEW YORK

Dedicated to the memory of

A. D. F. HAMLIN

Professor of Architectural History in Columbia
University and my first instructor in design,
in recognition of his faithful service to art, and
for his inspiring guidance in the appreciation
of fundamentals that made subsequent studies
a pleasure.

Published in Canada by General Publishing
Company, Ltd., 30 Lesmill Road, Don Mills,
Toronto, Ontario.
Published in the United Kingdom by Con-
stable and Company, Ltd., 10 Orange Street,
London WC 2.

This Dover edition, first published in 1946,
is a revised and enlarged version of the work
originally published by Harper and Brothers
in 1932.

Standard Book Number: 486-20125-2

Library of Congress Catalog Card Number: 46-4027

Manufactured in the United States of America

Dover Publications, Inc.
180 Varick Street
New York, N.Y. 10014

C O N T E N T S

III. THE TRIANGLE

IV. THE SQUARE

V. THE DIAMOND

F O R E W O R D

IN a world of changing taste one thing remains as a foundation for decorative design— the geometry of space division. Certain common symbolisms seem also to retain their vitality through the flux. Historical ornament as a basis of modern design, and any philosophy of taste based upon historic style consistency, are alike dead; we have come, in the decorative arts, to a period primarily of individual invention.

Few books exist which show an appreciation of the full implications of this fundamental change. After all, the geometry of space division can be analyzed into a comparatively small number of systems—an alphabet, as it were—and some contemporary presentation of this alphabet has long been needed. The commercial artist, the book-designer, the architect, the decorative painter, the designer of textiles—time and again they have sought in vain for such a reference work. This does not imply the need of a compendium of forms to copy blindly, but rather a collection of decorative shapes to stimulate the creative imagination. Necessarily, then, any such decorative alphabet must be of forms so abstracted and simplified as to be applicable to different types of design and susceptible of almost infinite variation. This alphabet Mr. Hornung has now compiled.

As a practical designer and for many years a student of decorative forms, the author is unusually well qualified. His well-known study of the trade-marks of the world has made him fully cognizant of the decorative potentialities of even the simplest forms, and given him as well a sure judgment in the choice, among the infinite number of geometric space divisions possible, of those most stimulating and most satisfactory. It is a pleasure to know that such a handbook has at last been made available.

TALBOT FAULKNER HAMLIN

COLUMBIA UNIVERSITY
JANUARY, 1932

PREFACE TO SECOND EDITION

A NEW FEATURE consisting of notes on the plates, has been included in this revised edition. This text has been purposely reduced to a set of brief references descriptive of some of the design elements that bear offhand resemblance to their neighbors. For instance, in the section treating of heraldic variants of the cross, these notes might easily be expanded into a full volume—in fact, entire books have appeared on this subject. But such an exhaustive study is not within the province of this book. The **Handbook** is essentially a source book for workers; those interested in further research will find the bibliography helpful in further pursuance of their studies.

It is obvious from the organic plan and arrangement of the plates, that the classification of designs is built upon the construction of the elements themselves, and not upon their symbolism. This approach may seem strange to many readers, but the author has chosen a geometric order deliberately. This, at least, is a known constant in a changing society where symbols, like nations, rise and fall. Some few years ago a clergyman found great delight, upon examination of this book, to note the large number of religious symbols included. On turning the pages further, his delight turned to horror as he came upon the plates dealing with the swastika—to him as to millions of others, a sign of bad repute in modern times. But the swastika, like so many other age-old symbols, has been alternately the omen of happiness or the sign of tyranny, depending upon whether civilizations have moved forward or backward in their course.

Looking back over the fifteen year period since work on this handbook was first begun, one is impressed with the many changes that have taken place in every field of human endeavor and industry—the field of fine and applied arts naturally included. Throughout these changing years there has been a consistent and increasing demand among students and practitioners alike—a demand far greater than could be met by the limited size of the first edition.

Whether because of newly trained men and women who have entered the applied arts, the opportunities ahead, or a renewed interest and appreciation of fundamental source material on the part of those already engaged in the field, the need is clearly indicative of a trend that fully justifies the author's original labors and the present publisher's willing cooperation. Whatever it is, it is hoped that this revised edition will become available to larger numbers than in the past, through the publisher's readiness to offer the work at a reduced price.

C. P. H.

NEW YORK, N. Y.
NOVEMBER 11, 1945

INTRODUCTION

HUNDREDS of volumes devoted to the study and application of design have been published during the last few decades, and thousands have appeared since the advent of printed books. The student, scholar, or practitioner visiting any well-equipped library is amazed at the vast amount of material that claims his attention; but upon investigation he will be disappointed to find how few of these books really meet his requirements. He will familiarize himself with the few compendia of ornament, such as Owen Jones' "Grammar of Ornament" and the "Ornement polychrome" of Racinet. These are monumental reference works, displaying their color plates according to comparative styles in art history. Dolmetsch's "Ornamental Treasure" and Speltz's "Styles of Ornament" are also useful. Unfortunately for the student of meager means, most of these volumes, since they are beyond the reach of his pocket, must be consulted on library shelves at infrequent intervals. It is a real pity that their merit is partially destroyed by their costliness.

Of art histories dealing with ornament and design there are comparatively few to interest the practical designer, although a number of exhaustive works have been published whose appeal is largely to the academician and archeologist. Hamlin's "History of Ornament," in two compact volumes, successfully summarizes the historic styles from ancient to modern times, and is designed particularly for student use. A great number of treatises on the meaning of design, form, and pattern have been issued, and they vary greatly in presentation from the conventional interpretation of Walter Crane to the highly personalized version of Claude Bragdon, or yet the free, modernized approach of Best-Maugard. In each of these the eager prospector will find much if he will but dig below the surface. Quite indispensable is Meyer's "Handbook of Ornament," which follows the synthetic rather than the analytic method, offering the elements with which to construct and develop ornament. But some forty years have passed since its first appearance in Germany, and the modern worker in applied arts still clings to it in the absence of a worthy successor.

Is it not strange, therefore, in a subject such as the study of design, enriched a thousandfold with the contributions of artist, author, architect, and archaeologist, that no single volume has placed before the modern designer the pure elements of decoration systematically arranged for quick and convenient reference? In his interest, this present handbook is undertaken.

The language of the designer, like the language of the writer, is vast in scope and complex in its ramifications. The communication of our thoughts by means of a written language constitutes a peculiar art which, like other arts, cannot be acquired in any degree of perfection, but by a complete mastery of the fundamental elements and by long-continued practice of their use. Some there are more highly endowed than others with a facility of expression, and naturally gifted with greater powers in the field of literature; but to none is it at all times an easy process to embody, in exact and appropriate language, the various ideas that are passing so swiftly through the mind. However distinct may be our views, however vivid our conceptions, we cannot but be conscious that the phraseology we have at our command is inadequate to do them justice. We seek in vain the words we need to portray our thoughts and sentiments. The appropriate terms, nothwithstanding our utmost efforts, cannot always be conjured up at will, and we are driven to the employment of a set of words and phrases either too general or too limited, too strong or too feeble, which miss the mark at which we aim.

To assist him in overcoming these deficiencies the writer has at his disposal the use of many aids—the grammar and rhetoric to correct his form and improve his composition, the dictionary to supply the true meanings of words, and the thesaurus to provide short-cuts to associated ideas and their means of expression. These, like the tools of any craftsman, are essential working instruments.

Let us consider the case of the designer. Let us observe how this analogy between writer and designer may be further drawn, by noting some major differences between the two. Instead of the writer's "twenty-six soldiers of lead to conquer the world," the designer has to command a bewildering array of simple character forms, geometric shapes, signs and strokes. In place of set and arbitrary rules for the combination of letters into word-forms, the designer has the freedom to modify existing forms, no matter how basic or fundamental. Should he choose to disregard convention, creating new motifs out of the fertility of his mind, only the degree of his own intelligence and ingenuity can limit resulting forms.

In this boundless realm of multitudinous shapes the designer is apt to find himself at sea. If he possesses rare collective faculties, a legion of thoughts will serve him in his greatest need. Others, less fortunate than he, must struggle to recall those many characters that constitute the designer's vocabulary. But to both skilled artist and novice, some reference to outside sources will be of benefit. Where shall one turn for such a grammar, or thesaurus of kindred forms?

● ● ●

In any handbook for ready reference, classification of material is of prime importance. The author's aim in devising the present plan was to obtain the greatest practical utility. Accordingly, such principles of arrangement were adopted as appeared simplest and most natural for organizing a heterogeneous mass of illustration. A necessarily arbitrary grouping follows, in the absence of any previous scientific classification, proceeding generally from simple to higher forms as indicated in the fifteen main divisions in the table of contents. Starting with the circle, for example, a number of examples are shown based upon variations in size, "color," subdivision, and combination. From the complete circle and its related arrangements, subdivisions into segments and sectors are next shown. And then follow devices in which circular forms are multiplied by integral relationship. This, broadly speaking, is the simple plan by which each element has been developed into a family of affiliated characters.

Certain designs, by nature of their construction, may be shown in one of several divisions. The triquetra, definitely tri-radial in form, is composed of circular arcs, and might be classified with circular variants. The guilloche, another rounded form, has been exhibited with the group of interlacements instead of circular variants. No hard and fast rule for these decisions has been followed except that of greatest useful-ness. Such a procedure, while hardly scientific and open to much criticism, is nevertheless a safe guide where quick ser-vice is a consideration. The author has had to face the alterna-tive of following a rigid academic outline, or a flexible one best suited to the purpose. Again, the designer's needs have dictated the author's course, and have controlled the final selection and sequence of plates.

In the selection of illustrations, it will be found that a greater variety of simple elements, such as the circle, square, and diamond, has been shown than of more complex forms. Essentially, the same principles of permutation and combina-tion will govern the multiplication of these higher forms; but rather than approach infinity with the number of designs shown, it has been deemed expedient to represent in greater variety only the simpler motifs shown in the earlier sections of the book. Repetition has been avoided, yet examples have been shown in sufficient number to stimulate thought and individual expression. Readers and critics may differ with the author in the judgment exercised; but he feels confident that if the lessons and principles of design which the many variations exhibit are studied diligently, the purpose of this volume will have been achieved.

Many of the examples may seem closely to resemble neighboring motifs. Where this is true it is suggested that the reader examine the respective devices, noticing particularly such changes in form as have been accomplished by an enlargement of one or another of its members, an outline treatment of some portion, or a reversal in "color" value. The author has treated of this last-named property at some length in the group of snow crystals. These pages are arranged in pairs, the right-hand side exhibiting a set of forms drawn black on white, the left showing its counterpart, white on black. The two groups show a negative and positive of the same motif and hence afford many interesting lessons for observation.

The use of over eighteen hundred illustrations appearing in this volume has resulted from a close study of those art cultures of the past wherein the geometric and abstract phase of design have been dominant. The arts of design in ancient Egypt, Greece, Arabia, and Japan have contributed liberally to the material upon which this work is based. Relatively few of the motifs are of the author's own invention. He has endeavored to present common property in a strictly impersonal way, relying more upon the order of presentation and system of arrangement for whatever claims to originality this work may possess. His greatest debt he acknowledges to that splendid system of Japanese heraldry that inspired this study, and without whose basis this handbook would still have been in its formative stage.

The matter of correct nomenclature has presented many unsuspected difficulties. The author has sought to give the proper terminology by which the many elements are known. It has been found that not only is there a wide divergence of opinion depending upon books consulted, but that in many cases there were no accepted terms whatever. This has served to impose an added burden of responsibility upon a task undertaken for other purposes, and the author has attempted solution of a vexatious problem in a most direct manner. As an illustration typical of the confusion met with let us examine the names for the common swastika. This motif is variously called sauvastika, tetraskele, fylfot, gammadion, and gammata. If one refers to Adeline's Art Dictionary, he will find no mention of swastika, since the popular English equivalent is the word fylfot. This condition becomes more trying as we seek to label forms of lesser usage. The triskele, triskelion, triquetra, triquetrum and trinacria, to cite one group, are hopelessly intermingled in their definitions in various books, and there is no final authority for the correct meanings. If the designations herein used do not meet with universal approval, it is hoped that some learned group will authorize a new dictionary of art terms that will set at rest the common misunderstanding that has existed for centuries.

●   ●   ●

A number of friends have very graciously assisted in the production of this volume. The author is especially indebted to Alexander Lindey and Albert Schiller for invaluable editorial aid, and to Talbot Hamlin for his kindly cooperation in supplying the foreword. Ordway Tead and Arthur Rushmore, representing the whole-hearted support of the publishers, by their helpful suggestions and patient endurance, have shared faithfully in the production of this work. Ernest Clement and Ryusaku Tsunoda of the Japanese Culture Center, Columbia University, have assisted with textual transcriptions of Japanese motifs. To all these and a score of willing craftsmen who have labored to fructify this work, the author extends his sincere appreciation.

C. P. H.

NEW YORK, N. Y.
OCTOBER 20, 1931

BIBLIOGRAPHY

ABSTRACT DESIGN

Bentley, Wilson, and Humphreys, William J., Snow Crystals

Best-Maugard, Adolfo, A Method for Creative Design

Bourgoin, J., Les éléments de l'art arabe

Bragdon, Claude F., Four Dimensional Vistas; Projective Ornament

Butler, G. M., Manual of Geometrical Crystallography

Christie, Archibald H., Traditional Methods of Pattern Designing

Crane, Walter, Bases of Design

Cutler, T. W., A Grammar of Japanese Ornament and Design

Day, Lewis F., Pattern Design; The Anatomy of Pattern

Fauré, P., La décoration géométrique

Fenn, Amor, Abstract Design

Hatton, R. G., Design—The Making of Patterns

Petrie, Flinders, Decorative Patterns of the Ancient World; Egyptian Decorative Art

Ross, Denman W., A Theory of Pure Design

Schauermann, François Louis, Theory and Analysis of Ornament

Sekai, Bijutsu, A World of Art (4 vols.)

HERALDRY

Cole, H., Heraldry and Floral Forms as Used in Decoration

Fox-Davies, A. C., Complete Guide to Heraldry

Hirashichi-Kotani, Book of Family Emblems, or Crests

Hope, W. H. St. John, Heraldry for Craftsmen and Designers

Rothery, G. C., The A B C of Heraldry

Stroehl, Hugo Gerard, Japanisches Wappenbuch

HISTORY AND COMPENDIA OF DESIGN

Dolmetsch, H., Ornamental Treasures
Glazier, Richard, Manual of Historic Ornament
Hamlin, A. D. F., History of Ornament (2 vols.)
Meyer, Franz Sales, Handbook of Ornament
Racinet, A., L'Ornement polychrome
Speltz, Alexander, Styles of Ornament
Ward, J., Historic Ornament

SYMBOLISM AND PHILOSOPHY OF DESIGN

Allen, Maude Rex, Japanese Art Motives
Alviella, d'Count Goblet, The Migration of Symbols
Arveat, L., Signes et symbols
Bailey, Henry Turner, and Pool, Ethel, Symbolism for Artists
Bragdon, Claude F., The Beautiful Necessity
Bragdon, Claude F., Projective Ornament
Brinton, Daniel G., The Taki, the Swastika and the Cross in America
Churchward, Albert, Signs and Symbols of Primordial Man
Edwards, Edward B., Dynamarhythmic Design
Goldsmith, Elizabeth E., Life Symbols
Haddon, Alfred C., Evolution in Art
Hambidge, Jay, Practical Applications of Dynamic Symmetry
Koch, Rudolph, Book of Signs
Rothery, G. C., Decorators' Symbols, Emblems, and Devices
Simpson, John Ward, The Gate Beautiful
Simpson, William, The Trisula Symbol
Webber, F. R., Church Symbolism

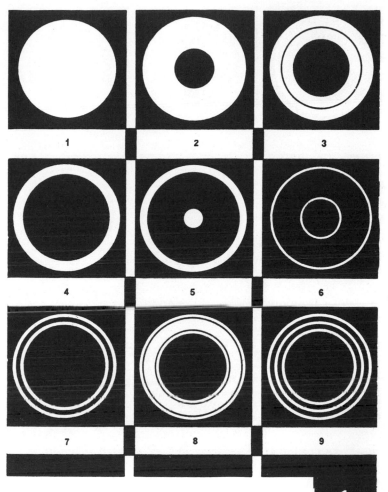

1

2

3

4

5

6

7

8

9

1

The Circle

10   11   12

13   14   15

16   17   18

The Crescent and Its Combinations

19

20

21

22

23

24

25

26

27

The Sector and Its Combinations

4

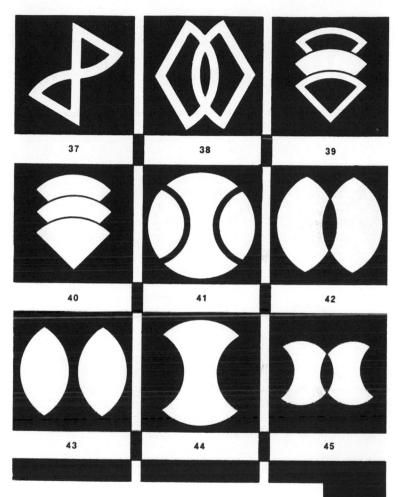

37 38 39

40 41 42

43 44 45

5

The Segment and Its Combinations

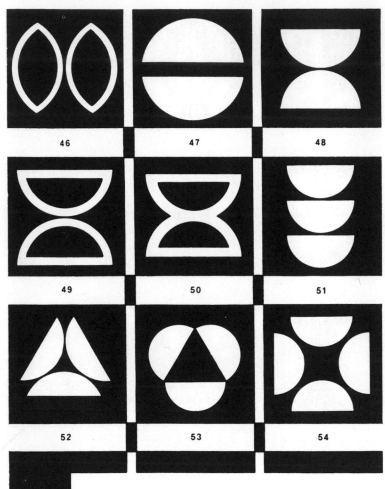

46

47

48

49

50

51

52

53

54

The Segment and Its Combinations

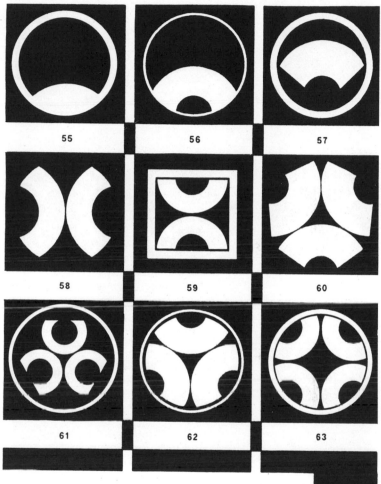

55

56

57

58

59

60

61

62

63

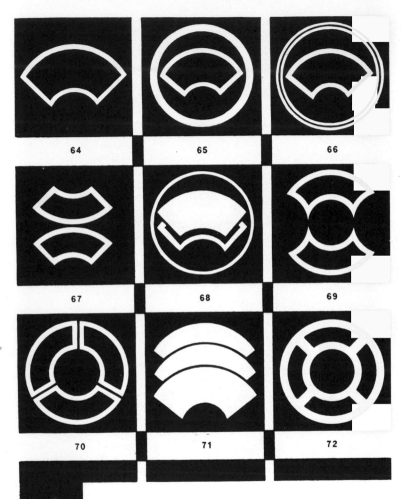

64 65 66

67 68 69

70 71 72

73

74

75

76

77

78

79

80

81

9

The Circle and Its Subdivision

91

92

93

94

95

96

97

98

99

11

The Circle and Its Combinations

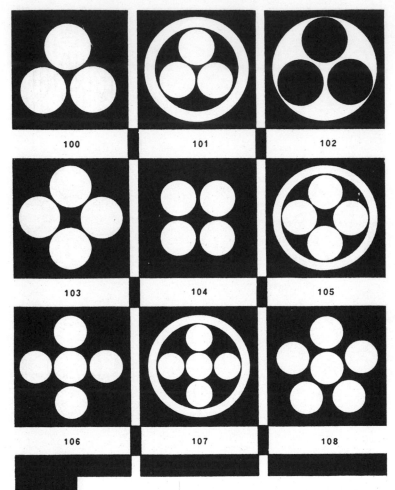

100

101

102

103

104

105

106

107

108

The Circle and Its Combinations

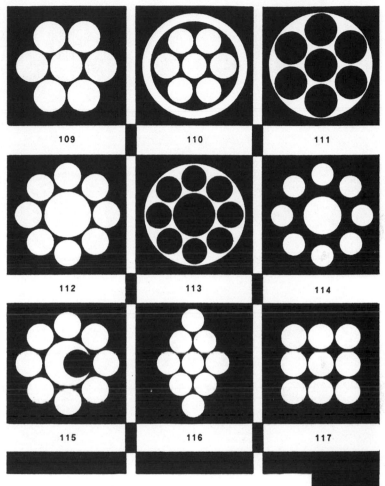

109   110   111

112   113   114

115   116   117

13

The Circular Variant

118

119

120

121

122

123

124

125

126

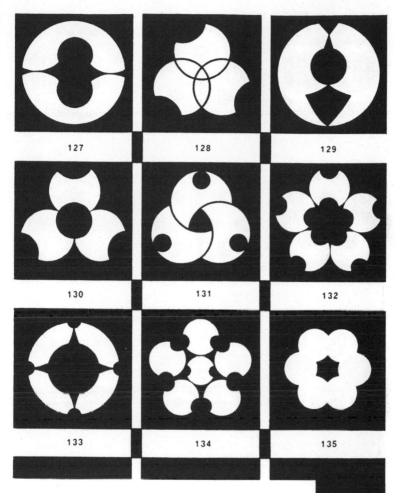

127 128 129

130 131 132

133 134 135

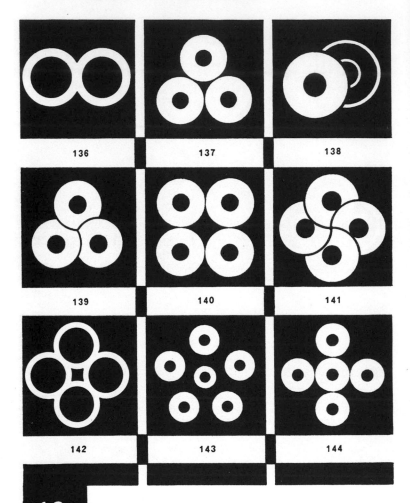

136

137

138

139

140

141

142

143

144

16

The Ringed Interlacement

154

155

156

157

158

159

160

161

162

163

164

165

166

167

168

169

170

171

The Ringed Interlacement

172

173

174

175

176

177

178

179

180

181   182   183

184   185   186

187   188   189

The Ringed Interlacement

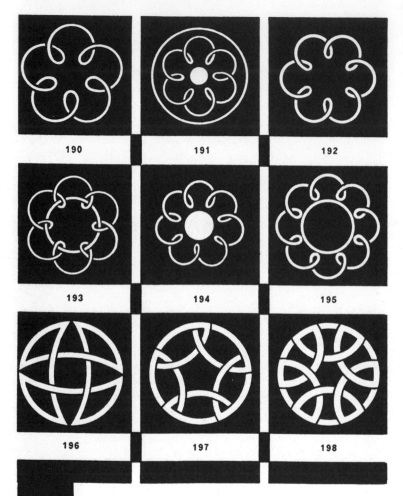

190

191

192

193

194

195

196

197

198

199

200

201

202

203

204

205

206

207

23

The Quatrefoil

208

209

210

211

212

213

214

215

216

24

The Line and Band

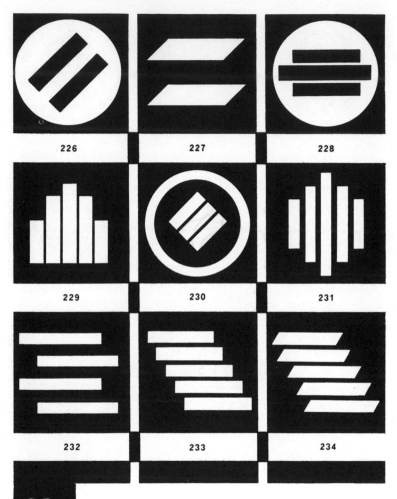

226   227   228

229   230   231

232   233   234

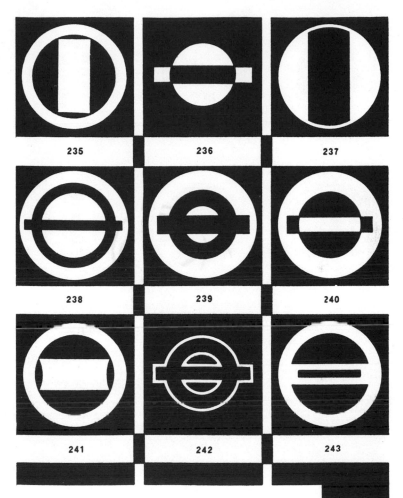

235

236

237

238

239

240

241

242

243

27

The Band Encircled

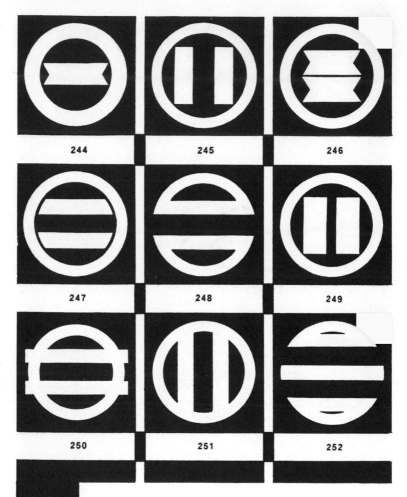

244

245

246

247

248

249

250

251

252

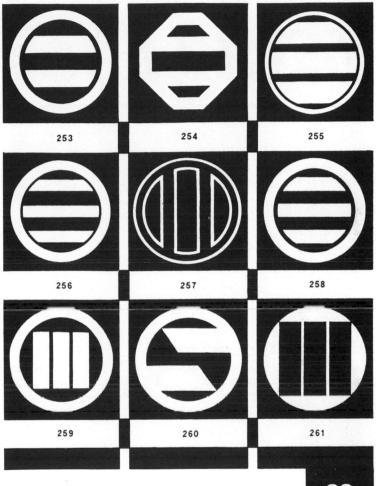

253 254 255

256 257 258

259 260 261

The Band Encircled

262   263   264

265   266   267

268   269   270

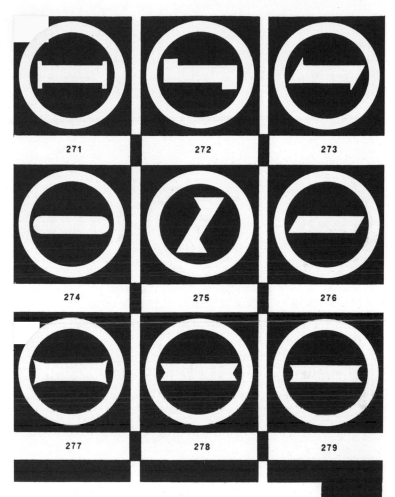

271

272

273

274

275

276

277

278

279

The Plaid

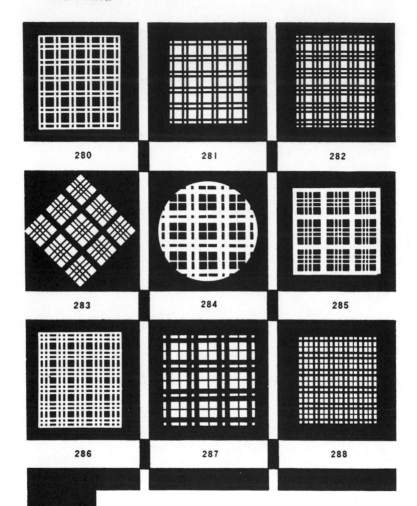

280

281

282

283

284

285

286

287

288

289

290

291

292

293

294

295

296

297

The Wavy Line

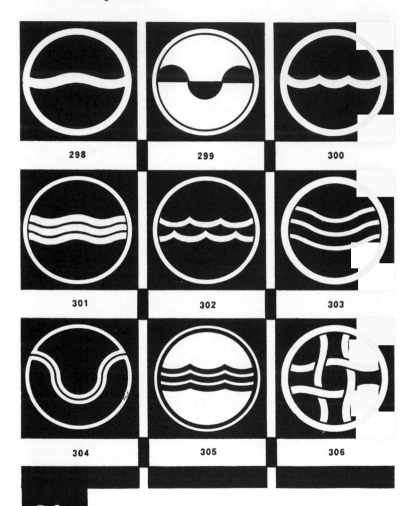

298

299

300

301

302

303

304

305

306

307   308   309

310   311   312

313   314   315

The Triangle

316

317

318

319

320

321

322

323

324

325

326

327

328

329

330

331

332

333

The Triangle and Its Combinations

334   335   336

337   338   339

340   341   342

The Triangle and Its Combinations

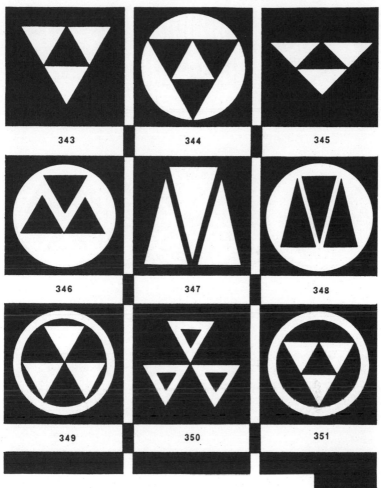

343

344

345

346

347

348

349

350

351

The Triangle and Its Combinations

352

353

354

355

356

357

358

359

360

The Triangle and Its Combinations

361   362   363

364   365   366

367   368   369

The Triangle and Its Combinations

370

371

372

373

374

375

376

377

378

The Triangle and Its Combinations

379

380

381

382

383

384

385

386

387

The Triangle and Its Subdivision

388

389

390

391

392

393

394

395

396

The Triangle and Its Subdivision

397

398

399

400

401

402

403

404

405

The Triangular Variant

415 416 417

418 419 420

421 422 423

The Double-triangular Variant

The Double-triangular Variant

433

434

435

436

437

438

439

440

441

The Arrow-head

442

443

444

445

446

447

448

449

450

The Arrow-head and Its Combinations

451   452   453

454   455   456

457   458   459

The Arrow-head and Its Combinations

460 461 462

463 464 465

466 467 468

The Arrow-tail and Its Combinations

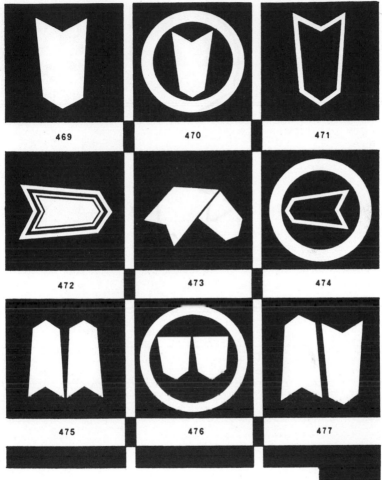

469

470

471

472

473

474

475

476

477

The Arrow-tail and Its Combinations

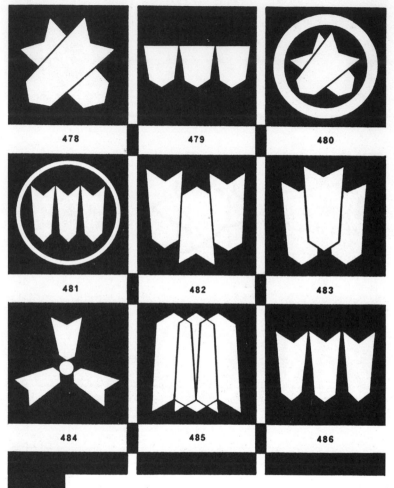

478
479
480
481
482
483
484
485
486

487   488   489

490   491   492

493   494   495

The Chevron and Its Combinations

496

497

498

499

500

501

502

503

504

The Chevron and Its Combinations

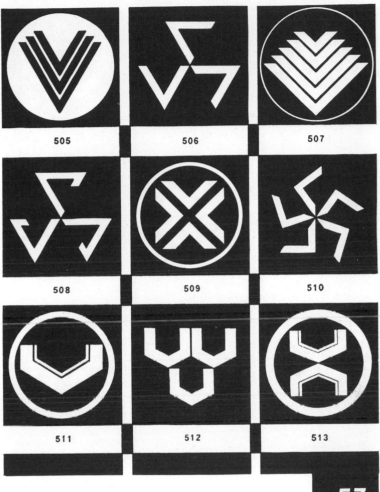

505

506

507

508

509

510

511

512

513

The Chevron and Its Combinations

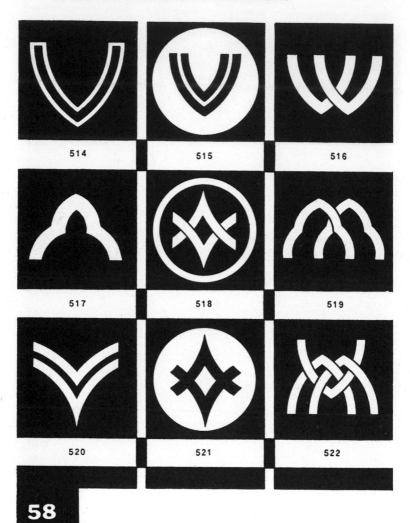

514

515

516

517

518

519

520

521

522

523

524

525

526

527

528

529

530

531

59

The Tri-radial Variant

541   542   543

544   545   546

547   548   549

The Tri-radial Variant

550

551

552

553

554

555

556

557

558

The Tri-radial Variant

559

560

561

562

563

564

565

566

567

The Triquetra

568

569

570

571

572

573

574

575

576

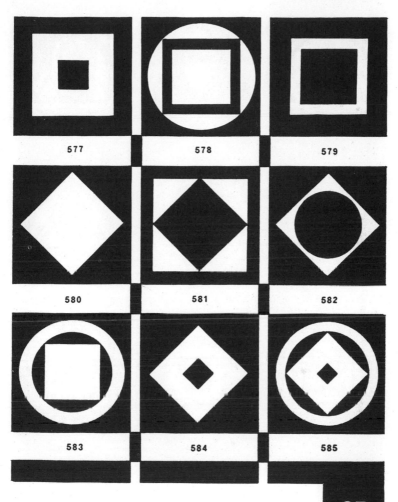

577 578 579

580 581 582

583 584 585

65

The Square

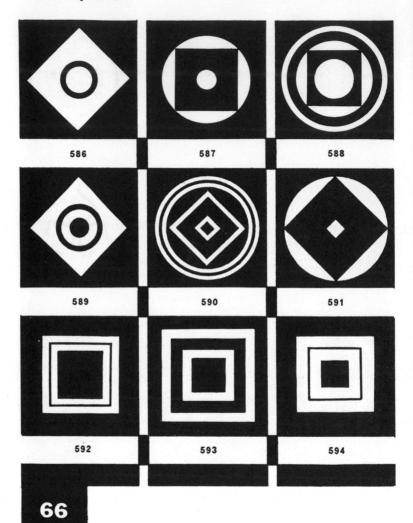

586

587

588

589

590

591

592

593

594

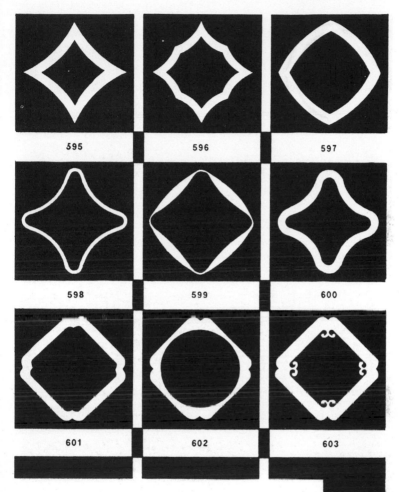

595 596 597

598 599 600

601 602 603

The Rectangular Variant

604

605

606

607

608

609

610

611

612

613

614

615

616

617

618

619

620

621

The Square and Its Combinations

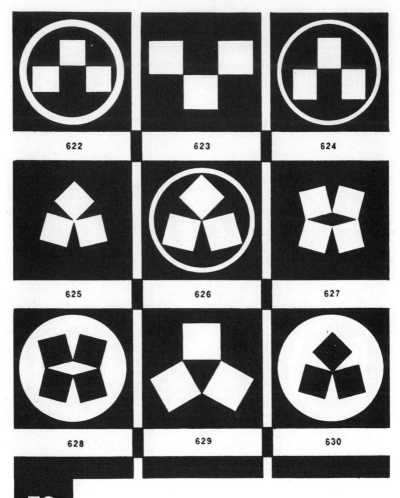

622

623

624

625

626

627

628

629

630

The Square and Checker Combinations

631 632 633

634 635 636

637 638 639

The Rectangular Combinations

640   641   642

643   644   645

646   647   648

The Rectangular Combinations

649

650

651

652

653

654

655

656

657

The Rectangular Combinations

658

659

660

661

662

663

664

665

666

The Rectangular Combinations

667

668

669

670

671

672

673

674

675

The Rectangular Combinations

676

677

678

679

680

681

682

683

684

The Rectangular Interlacement

685

686

687

688

689

690

691

692

693

The Rectangular Interlacement

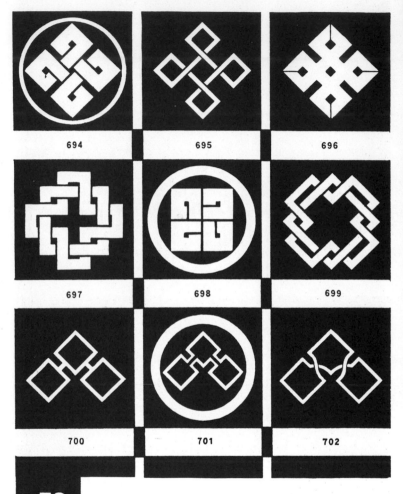

694

695

696

697

698

699

700

701

702

703

704

705

706

707

708

709

710

711

The Rectangular Form

712

713

714

715

716

717

718

719

720

721 722 723

724 725 726

727 728 729

The Rectangular Form

730

731

732

733

734

735

736

737

738

739

740

741

742

743

744

745

746

747

The Rectangular Form

748   749   750

751   752   753

754   755   756

757

758

759

760

761

762

763

764

765

The Diamond

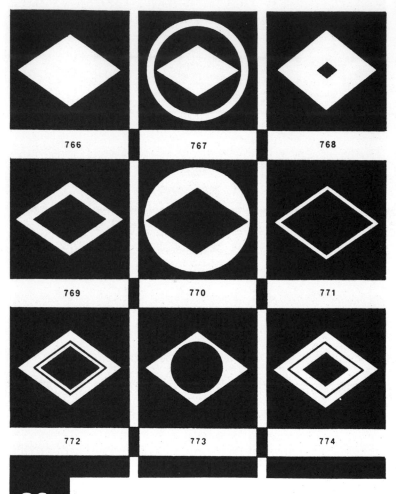

766 767 768

769 770 771

772 773 774

The Diamond and Its Variants

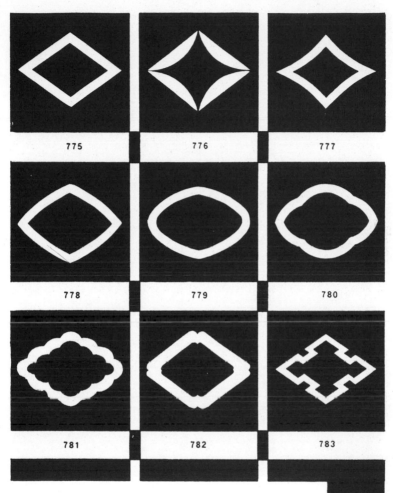

775

776

777

778

779

780

781

782

783

The Diamond and Its Combinations

784

785

786

787

788

789

790

791

792

The Diamond and Its Combinations

793

794

795

796

797

798

799

800

801

The Diamond and Its Combinations

802

803

804

805

806

807

808

809

810

The Rhombic Variant

820 821 822

823 824 825

826 827 828

829

830

831

832

833

834

835

836

837

The Rhombic Variant

838

839

840

841

842

843

844

845

846

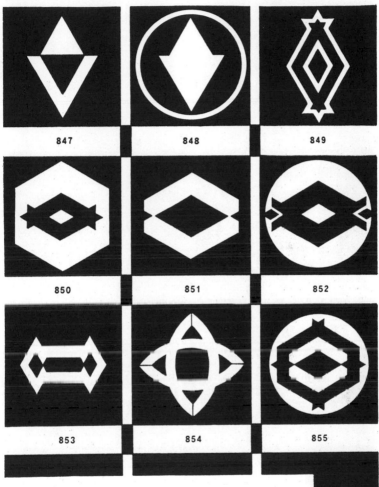

847 848 849

850 851 852

853 854 855

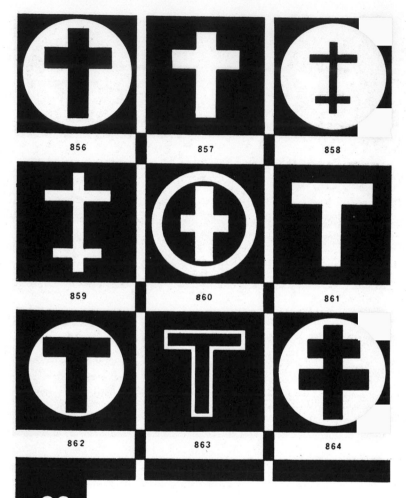

856 857 858

859 860 861

862 863 864

865

866

867

868

869

870

871

872

873

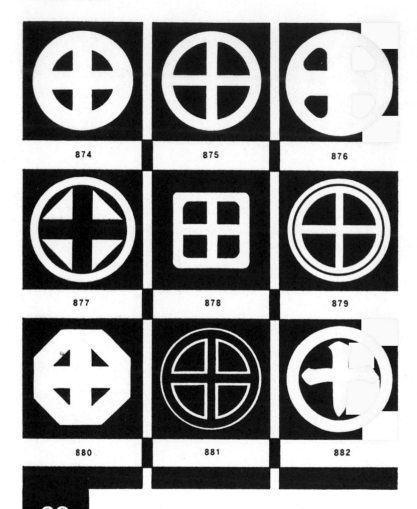

874

875

876

877

878

879

880

881

882

883   884   885

886   887   888

889   890   891

99

892

893

894

895

896

897

898

899

900

100

901

902

903

904

905

906

907

908

909

101

The Cross and Its Variants

910   911   912

913   914   915

916   917   918

919

920

921

922

923

924

925

926

927

928

929

930

931

932

933

934

935

936

937

938

939

940

941

942

943

944

945

The Cross and Its Variants

946

947

948

949

950

951

952

953

954

955

956

957

958

959

960

961

962

963

The Cross and Its Variants

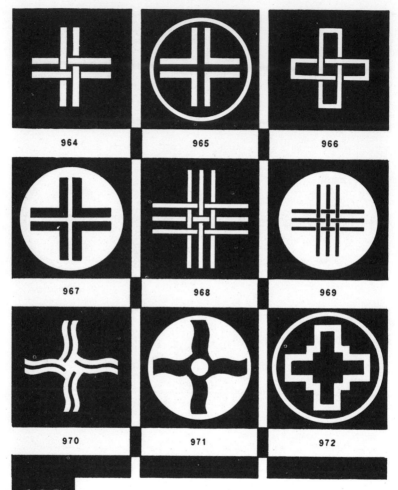

964

965

966

967

968

969

970

971

972

The Cross and Its Variants

973

974

975

976

977

978

979

980

981

109

982   983   984

985   986   987

988   989   990

991   992   993

994   995   996

997   998   999

111

The Cross and Its Variants

1000   1001   1002

1003   1004   1005

1006   1007   1008

1009 1010 1011

1012 1013 1014

1015 1016 1017

The Four-pointed Star, etc.

1018

1019

1020

1021

1022

1023

1024

1025

1026

1027   1028   1029

1030   1031   1032

1033   1034   1035

115

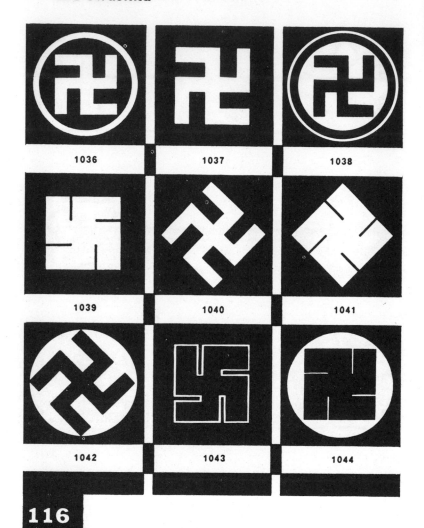

1036   1037   1038

1039   1040   1041

1042   1043   1044

The Swastika and Its Variants

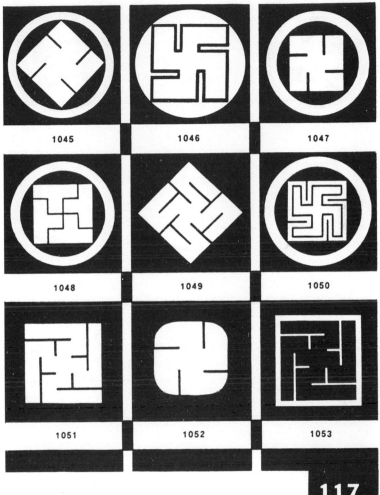

1045 1046 1047

1048 1049 1050

1051 1052 1053

The Swastika and Its Variants

1054 1055 1056

1057 1058 1059

1060 1061 1062

118

The Swastika and Its Combinations

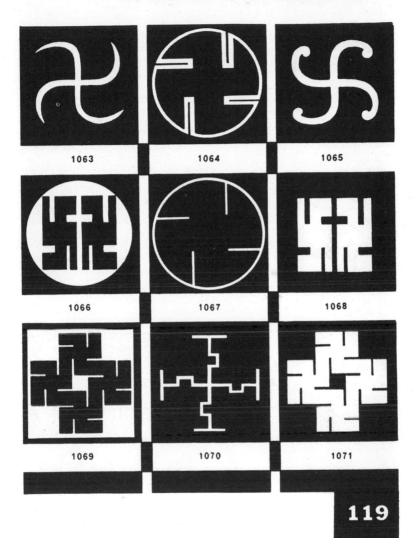

1063

1064

1065

1066

1067

1068

1069

1070

1071

The Swastika and Its Oblique Variants

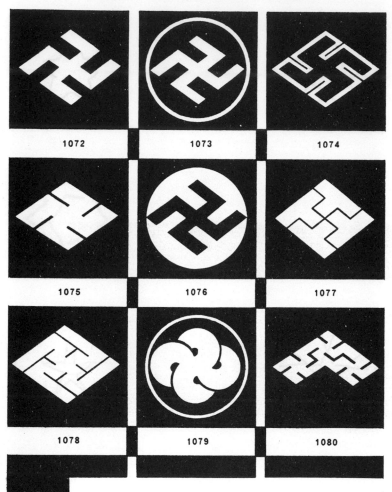

1072   1073   1074

1075   1076   1077

1078   1079   1080

1081   1082   1083

1084   1085   1086

1087   1088   1089

121

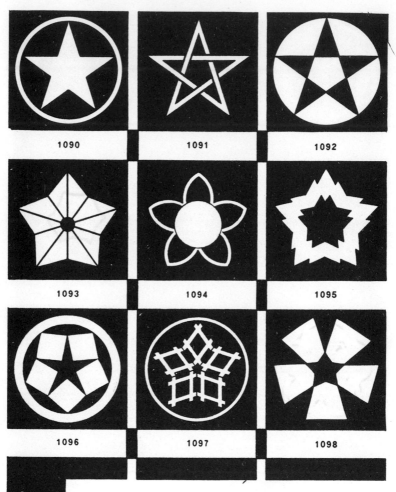

1090

1091

1092

1093

1094

1095

1096

1097

1098

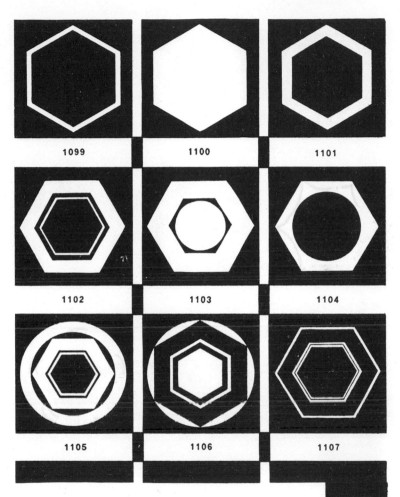

1099   1100   1101

1102   1103   1104

1105   1106   1107

The Hexagon and Its Variants

1108

1109

1110

1111

1112

1113

1114

1115

1116

124

The Hexagon and Its Combinations

1117

1118

1119

1120

1121

1122

1123

1124

1125

The Hexagon and Its Combinations

1126 1127 1128

1129 1130 1131

1132 1133 1134

The Hexagon and Its Combinations

1135

1136

1137

1138

1139

1140

1141

1142

1143

The Hexagonal Variant

1144

1145

1146

1147

1148

1149

1150

1151

1152

1153   1154   1155

1156   1157   1158

1159   1160   1161

129

The Hexagonal Variant

1162

1163

1164

1165

1166

1167

1168

1169

1170

1171	1172	1173
1174	1175	1176
1177	1178	1179

131

The Six-pointed Star

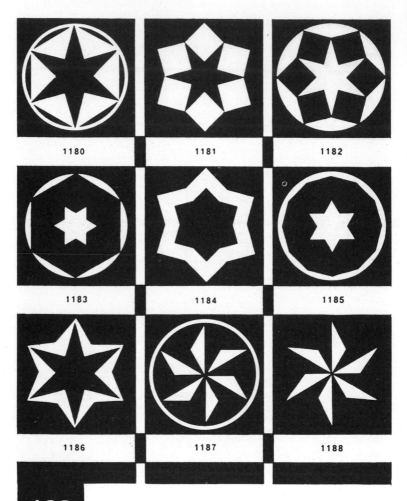

1180

1181

1182

1183

1184

1185

1186

1187

1188

1189   1190   1191

1192   1193   1194

1195   1196   1197

133

The Seal of Solomon

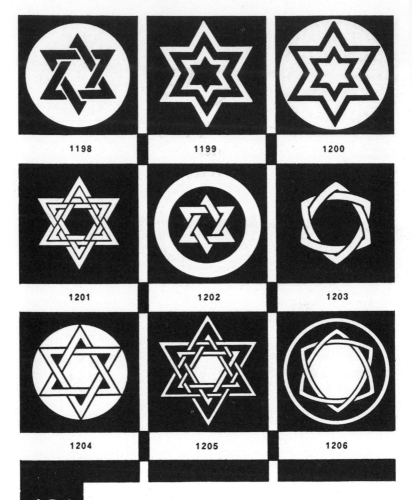

1198   1199   1200

1201   1202   1203

1204   1205   1206

The Hex-axial Variant

1207   1208   1209

1210   1211   1212

1213   1214   1215

The Hex-axial Variant

1216　　　　1217　　　　1218

1219　　　　1220　　　　1221

1222　　　　1223　　　　1224

1225

1226

1227

1228

1229

1230

1231

1232

1233

1234

1235

1236

1237

1238

1239

1240

1241

1242

1243

1244

1245

1246

1247

1248

1249

1250

1251

139

The Snow-crystal

1252

1253

1254

1255

1256

1257

1258

1259

1260

1261

1262

1263

1264

1265

1266

1267

1268

1269

The Snow-crystal

1270

1271

1272

1273

1274

1275

1276

1277

1278

142

1279

1280

1281

1282

1283

1284

1285

1286

1287

143

The Snow-crystal

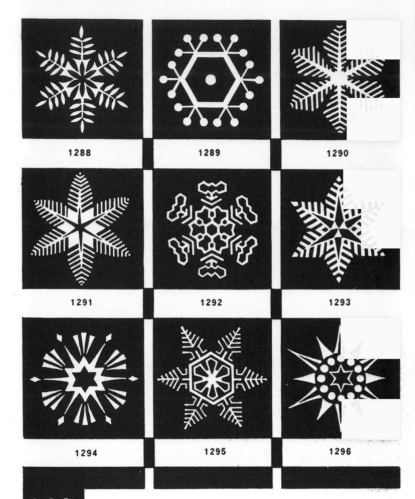

1288

1289

1290

1291

1292

1293

1294

1295

1296

144

1297

1298

1299

1300

1301

1302

1303

1304

1305

145

The Snow-crystal

1306 1307 1308

1309 1310 1311

1312 1313 1314

1315 1316 1317

1318 1319 1320

1321 1322 1323

The Octagon

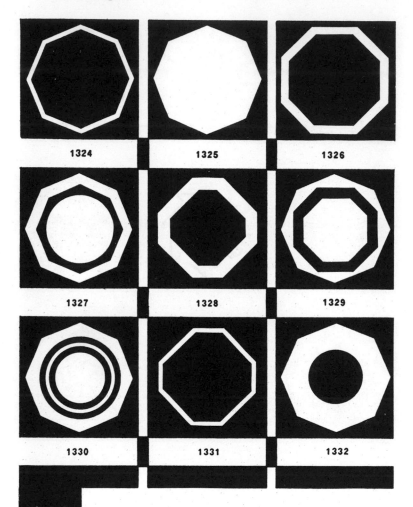

1324

1325

1326

1327

1328

1329

1330

1331

1332

1333

1334

1335

1336

1337

1338

1339

1340

1341

149

The Octagonal Form

1342   1343   1344

1345   1346   1347

1348   1349   1350

1351

1352

1353

1354

1355

1356

1357

1358

1359

151

The Octagram and Eight-pointed Star

1360

1361

1362

1363

1364

1365

1366

1367

1368

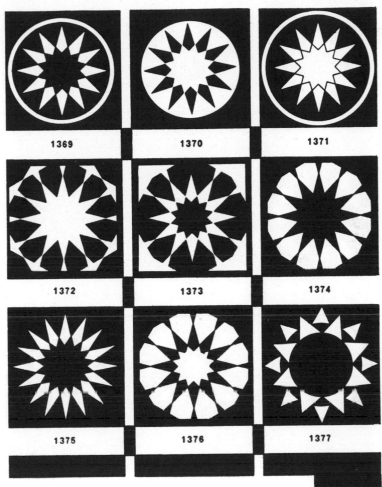

1369 1370 1371

1372 1373 1374

1375 1376 1377

The Solar Variant

1378

1379

1380

1381

1382

1383

1384

1385

1386

1387

1388

1389

1390

1391

1392

1393

1394

1395

The Scroll and Its Combinations

1396   1397   1398

1399   1400   1401

1402   1403   1404

1405   1406   1407

1408   1409   1410

1411   1412   1413

157

The Scroll and Its Combinations

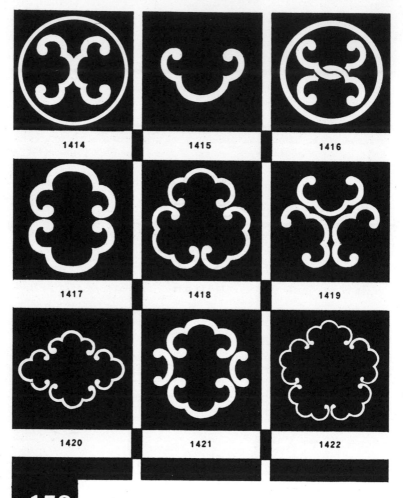

1414

1415

1416

1417

1418

1419

1420

1421

1422

1423 1424 1425

1426 1427 1428

1429 1430 1431

The Spiral Scroll and S-scroll

1432

1433

1434

1435

1436

1437

1438

1439

1440

The Triskelion and Tetraskelion

The Scroll-form and Its Combinations

1459   1460   1461

1462   1463   1464

1465   1466   1467

The Wave Scroll

1468

1469

1470

1471

1472

1473

1474

1475

1476

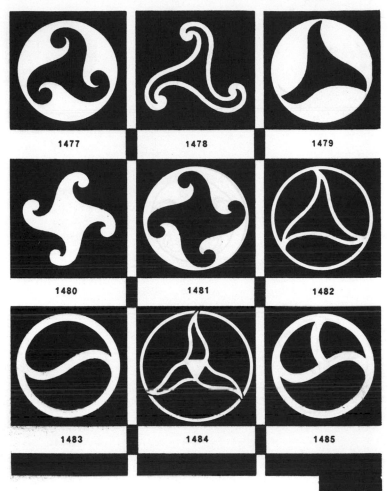

1477

1478

1479

1480

1481

1482

1483

1484

1485

165

The Monad and Its Variants

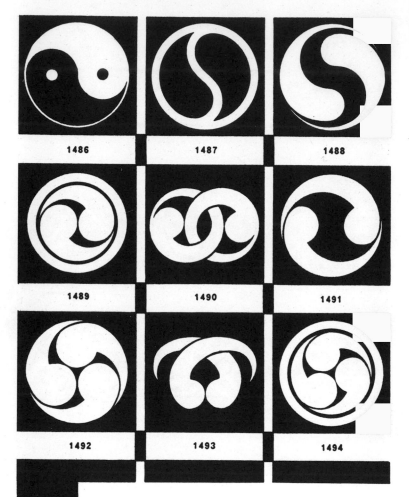

1486   1487   1488

1489   1490   1491

1492   1493   1494

The Triad and Its Variants

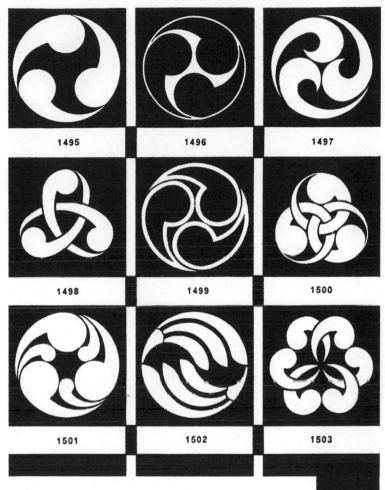

1495   1496   1497

1498   1499   1500

1501   1502   1503

The Circular Enclosure

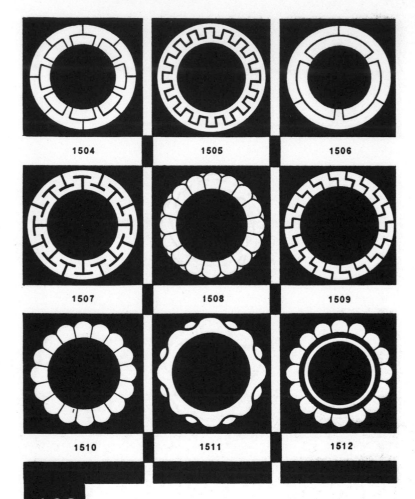

1504

1505

1506

1507

1508

1509

1510

1511

1512

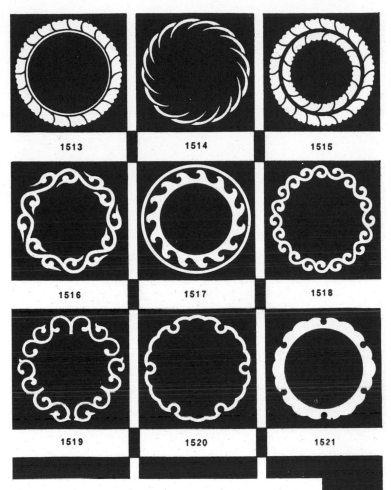

1513

1514

1515

1516

1517

1518

1519

1520

1521

The Curvilinear Variant

1522

1523

1524

1525

1526

1527

1528

1529

1530

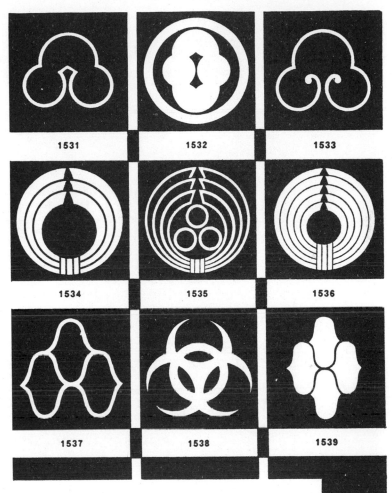

The Loop and Guilloche

1540

1541

1542

1543

1544

1545

1546

1547

1548

1549   1550   1551

1552   1553   1554

1555   1556   1557

173

The Curvilinear Interlacement

1558   1559   1560

1561   1562   1563

1564   1565   1566

The Interlacement and Its Variants

1567

1568

1569

1570

1571

1572

1573

1574

1575

175

The Interlacement and Its Variants

The Rectangular Interlacement

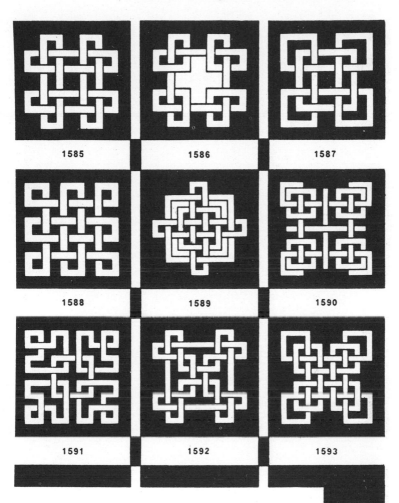

1585   1586   1587

1588   1589   1590

1591   1592   1593

The Angular Interlacement

1594

1595

1596

1597

1598

1599

1600

1601

1602

1603

1604

1605

1606

1607

1608

1609

1610

1611

The Fret and Its Variants

1612

1613

1614

1615

1616

1617

1618

1619

1620

The Fret and Its Variants

1621   1622   1623

1624   1625   1626

1627   1628   1629

The Fret and Its Variants

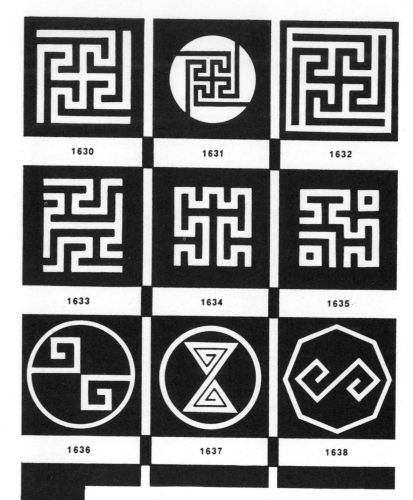

1630   1631   1632

1633   1634   1635

1636   1637   1638

The Fret and Its Combinations

1639   1640   1641

1642   1643   1644

1645   1646   1647

The Fret and Its Combinations

1648　　　　1649　　　　1650

1651　　　　1652　　　　1653

1654　　　　1655　　　　1656

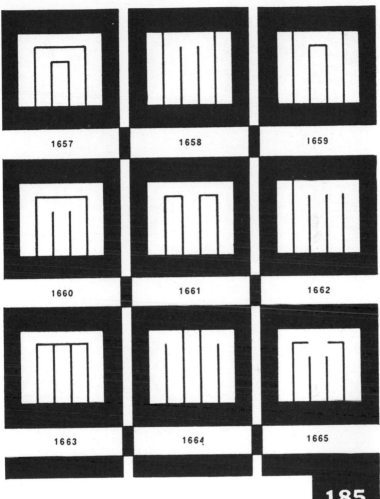

1657

1658

1659

1660

1661

1662

1663

1664

1665

185

The Rectangular Subdivision

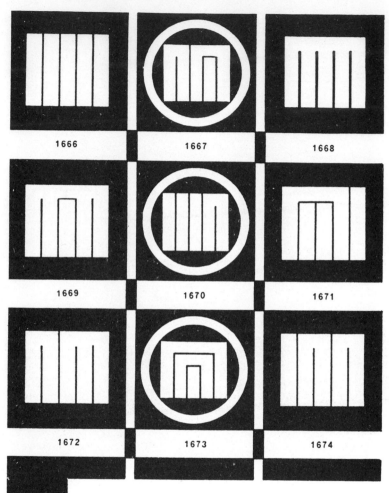

1666   1667   1668

1669   1670   1671

1672   1673   1674

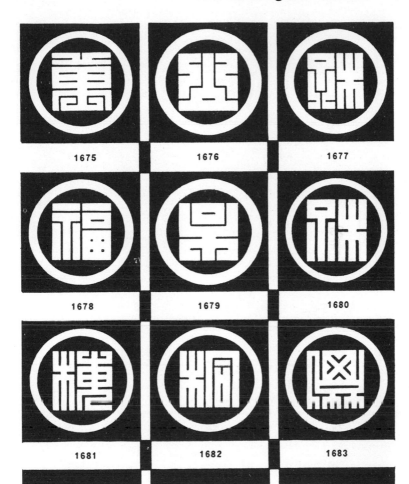

1675   1676   1677

1678   1679   1680

1681   1682   1683

The Rectangular Variant

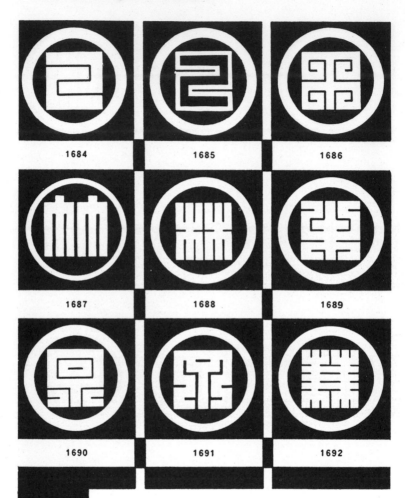

1684

1685

1686

1687

1688

1689

1690

1691

1692

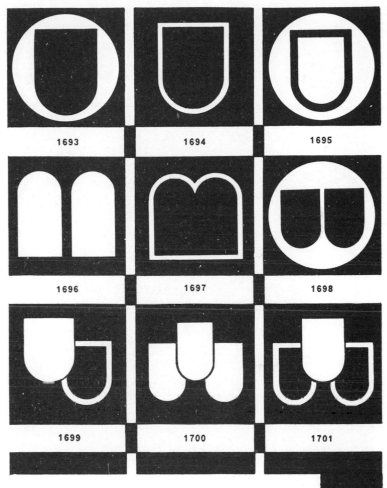

1693   1694   1695

1696   1697   1698

1699   1700   1701

The Shield and Its Variants

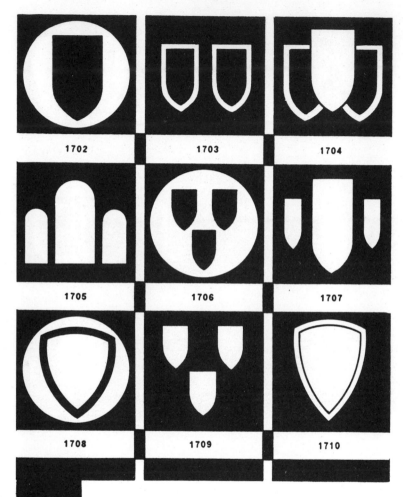

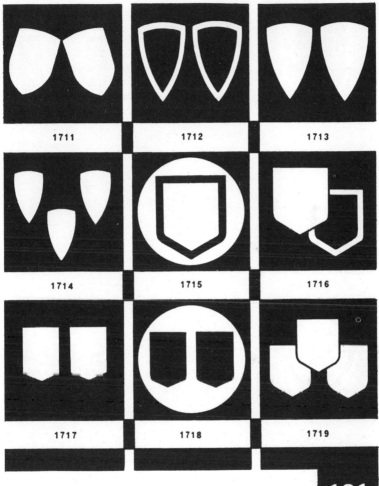

1711 1712 1713

1714 1715 1716

1717 1718 1719

The Shield and Its Variants

1720

1721

1722

1723

1724

1725

1726

1727

1728

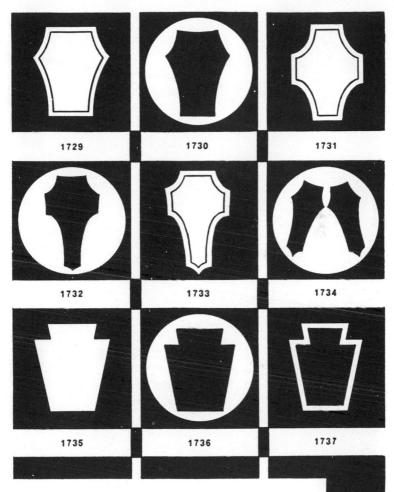

1729   1730   1731

1732   1733   1734

1735   1736   1737

The Shield and Its Subdivisions

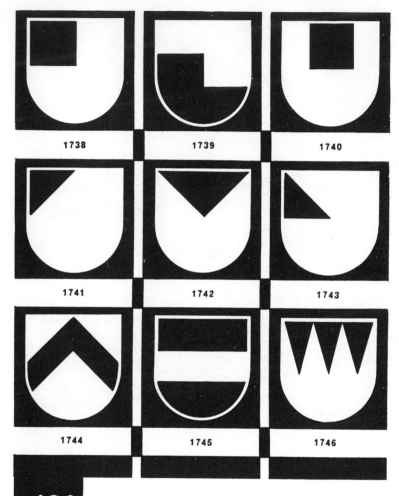

1738   1739   1740

1741   1742   1743

1744   1745   1746

The Shield and Its Subdivisions

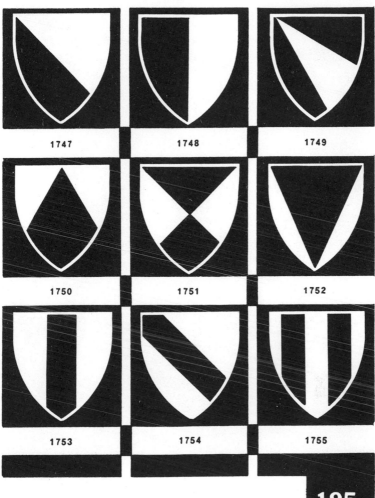

1747   1748   1749

1750   1751   1752

1753   1754   1755

The Shield and Its Subdivisions

1756   1757   1758

1759   1760   1761

1762   1763   1764

1765

1766

1767

1768

1769

1770

1771

1772

1773

The Shield and Its Subdivisions

1774   1775   1776

1777   1778   1779

1780   1781   1782

The Shield and Its Subdivisions

1792

1793

1794

1795

1796

1797

1798

1799

1800

The Shield and Its Subdivisions

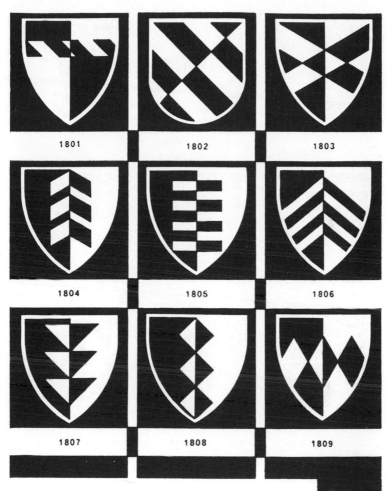

1801

1802

1803

1804

1805

1806

1807

1808

1809

The Shield and Its Subdivisions

1810

1811

1812

1813

1814

1815

1816

1817

1818

The Shield and Its Subdivisions

1819   1820   1821

1822   1823   1824

1825   1826   1827

1828

1829

1830

1831

1832

1833

1834

1835

1836

NOTES ON THE PLATES

The Circle. Plates 1-15. The circle is the simplest and most fundamental of all geometric shapes. Defined as a continuous, curved line, every point of which is equidistant from a central point, it forms the basis of an infinite number of shapes, forms, and patterns. By a process of multiplication, subdivision, and interlacement it is possible to produce devices in endless variety. These may well serve as a basis for combination with other shapes.

The subdivision of the circle is generally accomplished by the use of straight lines, or arcs, or any combination of these.

The Sector. The sector is that portion of a circle enclosed between two radii and the arc subtended.

The Quadrant. When the radii are at right angles the portion contained is called a quadrant.

The Segment. The segment is that portion of a circle enclosed between a straight line or chord, and the arc subtended.

The Crescent. When two circles intersect, as in Fig. 18, the exterior portions are called crescents, and the interior portion converging between two circular arcs is called a cissoid.

By describing circles that overlap one another, as in Figs. 91-97, and by describing circles to intersect each other, as in Figs. 73-90, 98, and 99, interesting variations can be obtained. In some cases the overlapped portions have been treated in black, resulting in a reversal of color called counterchange. Figs. 76 and 78 are simple examples of this device.

The circular form occurs frequently in nature. The sun, the moon in its varying phases, the constellations, the rainbow, annular rings, the pearl, the sunflower, the orange, the berry, and concentric ripples in still water are but a few of the most common manifestations.

Being without beginning or end, the circle has always symbolized eternity. It is also a symbol for the feminine principle in nature, completeness and perfection. In varying forms it is interpretative of the four elements: with a dot in the center it represents air; with a horizontal dividing line it represents water; with a cross dividing it into quarters it represents the earth; of itself it represents fire. From earliest times, because of its solar significance, it has been used by the savage and primitive to denote spiritual power. The Egyptian hieroglyph of the sun god was a point within a circle—Fig. 5. This most sacred device of the sun worshiper may have typified the seed within the egg, the "orphic egg," symbol of the universe, representing the globe of the sun floating in space surrounded by the enclosing vault of the heavens. A point within a circle is still in use today as the astronomical sign for the sun.

The Ring. Plates 16-22. The use of rings or annulets, either superimposed, interwoven, or interlaced, gives rise to an infinity of design. Common to most art cultures, their origin no doubt may be traced to the early use of ringed bracelets and anklets worn for personal adornment. The circular chain was also a source of inspiration for the fascinating combinations that have been handed down through the ages. Three circles, of equal size, but interlaced, as in Figs. 160-165, were used early in the history of the Christian church to symbolize the Holy Trinity. Each circle is complete in itself, and at the same time shares a common portion with the other two circles. This central point is the heart of the symbol of trinity, and suggests the divine essence.

As we multiply the number of circles involved, the effect is that of a rosette, or petular formation, as in Fig. 185. Some of the figures displayed, as Figs. 170, 171, 187-189, are not true ringed forms, but their development is so obvious that they have been included as interesting examples. The forms on Plate 22 also spring from the same sources.

The Trefoil. Plates 23-25. The cloverleaf, or club form, called the trefoil (from "trèfle" in French) is seen in Fig. 200. It is another symbol of the idea of trinity, and is formed of three lobes of equal size, yet one figure. The rims of these three circles, one above and two below, suggest the threefold aspect of life. Another variant of the trefoil contains an equilateral triangle enclosed, Figs. 199, 201, and 202, and still another is seen in Fig. 204, resulting from the combination of the trefoil and triangle by eliminating the interior lines.

The Quatrefoil. The quatrefoil, or four-lobed figure, resembles the "lucky" shamrock. It is formed by the intersection of the arcs of four circles, which may also be tangential, as in Fig. 216. In Fig. 211 a square has been interposed, and the interior lines eliminated.

The Cinquefoil. The cinquefoil, or five-lobed figure, Figs. 221 and 222, is a common decorative form since it resembles the five-foiled flower so frequently found in nature. In Figs. 223, 224, and 225 the six-pointed forms result from a double trefoil interlaced.

The Line and Band. Plates 26-31. A line, theoretically considered, and defined, is the result of projecting a dot in a given direction. It may be long or short, broad or narrow. But as the line increases in width, according to definition, it ceases to be a line and becomes an area. It is then called a band or stripe.

We shall disregard the true line in our present consideration, and be concerned with the properties and possibilities of the band. Lines may vary in direction. If they change their direction abruptly they become angular; if they change gradually, they become curved. The line may combine both of these characteristics and assume shapes of infinite variety.

The relationship of bands shown in Plate 26 may be varied, depending upon number, size, position, and termination. By placing these line groups into enclosures, as in Fig. 230, the character of the device may further be changed. In Plates 27-30 the band is shown in conjunction with the circle. Note how these designs supplement the circular variants shown in Plates 4 and 6.

The Plaid. Plate 32. The plaid is a pattern created by regularly spaced bands at right angles to one another. The resultant checkered effects may be endless in variety, depending upon the relationship and intervals between lines and bands. Where color is available, an infinity of patterns are the result. In Scotland, by means of an elaborate heraldry in plaid patterns, also called tartans, the Highland clans are variously represented.

The Lattice. Plate 33. The lattice, or basket weave, is the result of bands crossing over and under one another, either rectangularly or diagonally. The interlaced, all-over pattern may be varied by width of band, spacing, and alternation of band members.

The Wavy Line. Plate 34. The wavy line, Figs. 298 and 301, is formed by a succession of undulating, or elongated S curves. Fig. 300, another form usually associated with the wavy line, is shaped by a continuous and concurrent series of small semi-circles, or scallops, conjoined to each other. In heraldry, the former is called wavy, or undy, the latter engrailed, or invected. Both forms are obviously derived from water movements and have long been symbolical of it.

The Zigzag Line. Plate 35. The zigzag line is a regularly broken line, formed by angles which alternately project and retreat. In heraldry it is called indented, or dancette. It is one of the oldest and most persistent forms known to the decorative arts, and has always been considered a conventionalization of water. In Egyptian hieroglyphics it is the character sign for water.

The Triangle. Plates 36-45. The triangle is a plane, geometric figure having three sides and three angles. The equilateral triangle, Figs. 316-318, has three equal sides and angles, and is most useful in the decorative arts. The isosceles triangle, Figs. 319 and 320, has only two equal sides and angles, and may, from the standpoint of design, be considered as an equilateral triangle that has been extended in one direction. Only the equilateral triangle has been used in displaying variations and subdivisions. Obviously, in an isosceles triangle the same changes can be wrought. Resultant effects will then become a distortion of the equilateral variants.

While the characteristics of the triangle have been studied very precisely from the earliest times and many mathematical theorems expounding its properties have been proven, it is not easy to define its many complicated meanings and applications. It is so mysteriously involved as a potent life symbol that it is both complex and uncompromising. Basically it represents three things, one above two, the two lower uniting to produce the higher, and thus it symbolizes the union of positive and negative forces, the Law of Life. The ancients seem to have grasped the idea of trinity—the threefold nature of the universe—the divine, the human, and the natural world. The triangle, very naturally, was the simplest form to express this conception, although many variants have evolved from it. The persistence of the triangle, then, from the earliest scribblings of primordial man, may be ascribed to the growth and acceptance of the trinity concept: the family idea—father, mother, and child; or again, the metaphysical idea—body, mind, and spirit, which find their graphic symbol in the triangle. In Egypt the form signified the feminine principle, or maternity, and was also the hieroglyph for the moon. To the Pythagoreans it was the symbol for wisdom, and to the Babylonians it represented the triad division of the universe, heaven, earth, and air. The triangle has been used so extensively in all ages and countries that to catalogue its many interpretations would go beyond the scope of these brief notes.

Figs. 349, 350, and 355, consisting of three triangles touching at a central point, represent an ancient symbol for the Godhead. It has no authentic name, however. In Fig. 358, where three triangles overlap, the forms seem to project from the surface of the plane and take on a third dimension. Figs. 382 and 384, each consisting of five scalene triangles grouped about a central point, exhibit a definite suggestion of rotary motion; compared to these, notice how static the symmetrical devices appear. Fig. 386, consisting of six equilateral triangles arranged about a hexagon, resembles Solomon's Seal. (See Plate 134.)

Plate 44. When the triangle is divided into three equal parts by placing the Y fork, or furca, over the midway points of the sides, as in Figs. 388-393, three quadrilateral forms result. By placing the fork over the three angles, as in Figs. 391, 393, 394, and 396, three isosceles triangles result.

The Triangular Variant. Plates 46-49. An important triangular variant is produced in Plate 46 by making the sides convex, and in Plate 47, Figs. 415-417, by making the sides concave. In Figs. 418-421 the three-pointed star is produced by indenting the triangular sides.

In Plates 48 and 49, by placing two equilateral triangles end to end and overlapping the apexes slightly, a new form is produced with all the properties of the triangle. It resembles a conventionalization of the hourglass. In Figs. 427-429 it is seen with a crossbar through the center, a familiar figure to be found in Japanese family badges. Fig. 431 is an ancient Saracenic talisman in which the upper triangle represented the water triangle of kindness and nobility, while the lower one, the fire and the wrath of God.

The Arrow-head. Plates 50-52. The arrow-head, while not a pure geometric form, has all the characteristics and properties of the triangular motif. A number of variants are shown on Plate 50, and combinations of these on Plates 51 and 52. The arrow-head has been in use since early times, in decorations by the savage and his civilized successor. Originally it was associated with the idea of warfare, or to mark direction, but in later usage its pictographic significance was lost.

The Arrow-tail. Plates 53 and 54. The arrow-tail, or feather-tail, like the preceding motif, does not strictly conform to the triangular classification, but has, for practical uses, an interest in its present position. The arrow-tail is an irregular polygon derived from a conventionalization of the feather-tail. It also resembles the semaphore signal. The examples shown are based upon Japanese family crests.

The Chevron. Plates 55-58. The chevron is a simple, symmetrical V shape that may be regarded as an equilateral or isosceles triangle in which the third side has been removed. The chevron, repeated, bordered, interlaced, and diapered has always been a useful motif in surface decoration. In British and French heraldry it is the ordinary most popularly used, and has many variant forms. The term is derived from the French word, chevron, meaning a rafter, or gable. Most generally, the angle of the chevron is between 60 and 75 degrees, although there is no definition to prevent freedom in its shape. Since the Middle Ages, when house and holding marks developed so extensively, the chevron, because of its ease in marking and application to material, has been used to designate ownership and rank. Its military significance on uniforms, Fig. 520, is probably an outgrowth of this early usage.

As a form frequent in Japanese heraldry, Figs. 492, 493, and 496, it represents a mountain in profile.

The Triangular Form. Plate 59. These figures represent but a few simple variants built upon a triangular basis, whose number and possibility of variation are endless. The conforming shape is triangular, as are most of the resultant parts. Rhombic and star forms are produced in the details, as in Figs. 529 and 531, where the triangular forms overlap.

The Tri-radial Variant. Plates 60-63. Three is the smallest number of radiating axes by which an area or enclosure can be divided. It gives rise to a number of devices, shown on Plate 60, similar in form to those already encountered in Plates 44, 52. On Plate 61, is shown another tri-radial group possessing a strong suggestion of rotary motion. The triquetrum, Figs. 541-543, achieves this by following the skirl form based upon a number of curved radii facing in one direction. The wheel is one of the oldest symbols of the occult power of the sun. Among the Hindus and Buddhists the turning of the wheel represented rebirth. The rays of the wheel uniting in a common centre symbolized divine unity.

On Plate 62, Figs. 550, 551, and 553, are shown variants of a form called the sign of Trinacria. Originally derived from three triangles whose third side had been removed, this figure is another excellent example of motion achieved around a central point. A later evolution of this ancient symbol develops three revolving legs, but it is interesting to note that the plain geometrical figure precedes the swing to realism.

The Triquetra. Plate 64. The triquetra is a mystical three-pointed motif derived from three equal arcs of circles arranged in continuous fashion. It is simple in form, ingenious in design and full of significance. It is a symbol of Trinity, expressing the unity of divine essence, eternity, and indivisibility. Each pair of arcs forms a vesica, the symbol of glory.

The Square. Plates 65-69. The square is a rectilinear figure having four equal sides and four right angles. It may be divided in many ways: diagonally, it yields either two or four right angle triangles; laterally, through the mid-portions of the sides, it yields four squares. It may be variously divided by means of arcs and angles. A study of the properties of the square is best obtained by a study of its component parts, principally, the triangle. For this reason, the square seldom enters into the theorems of plane geometry.

The square is the simplest form in which bi-symmetric arrangements can be observed; as such it is related to the most important of bi-axial motifs, the cross. The square inscribed within the circle, Figs. 578, 583, 585, etc., and the square circumscribing the circle, as in Fig. 582, gives evidence of a strong fraternity between these two primal geometric forms.

The variants to be found on Plates 67 and 68 are familiar to all. They suggest with what ease the quadrilateral form may be generated into figures of interest and variety. These, as well as practically the entire group of rectangular variants and combinations, are derived from Japanese heraldry.

The applications of the square, and its manifold interpretations, are as varied as the form itself. It is a worldly figure and is emblematic of the four corners of the earth. Hence, in the Buddhist stupa, representing the elements of the universe, the square, or earth form, constitutes the base upon which all the others rest. Its host of meanings include: the elements, the heavens, the four Evangelists, the four points of the compass. It has entered into the colloquial language to a greater extent than any other geometric form. Thus, we refer to "four square," "fair and square," doing business "on the square," and "squaring up" one's accounts. The rigid uprightness of the square has become a beautiful symbol, much readier of comprehension than most other decorative elements.

On Plate 69, Figs. 616-618, and on Plate 76, Figs. 676, 677, and 679, are to be found squares that have been divided diagonally so that the triangular parts are quite obvious. These figures are based upon Japanese conventionalizations of the rice measure. On Plates 77 and 78 are a number of devices in which open squares are interlaced with one another. It is a characteristic of the interlacement that its line is continuous, and that in its successive overlappings it first goes over and then under the secondary member. Figs. 694, 695, 697, and 698 are worth special study for the variations that are obtained through weight of line or band. Fig. 698, while belonging generally to this group, is not so typical of the interlacement since its compact form destroys the usual properties of the interlacement.

On Plate 72 will be found a number of devices composed of rectangular forms. Figs. 640-642, each, consist of two rectangles placed over one another. Fig. 643 is derived from five squares of diminishing size, each inscribed obliquely within its next larger one. Figs. 646-648 result from four or eight squares overlapping and generating from a central point. In the four-combinations, a swastika is to be seen at the center.

On Plates 80-82 are some rectangular forms based upon an ancient Japanese device to be found in heraldry. It is a conventionalization of the well-frame, and is an excellent example of how well the Japanese can produce an abstract figure based upon common forms.

The Cross. Plates 96-113. When two lines cross each other at right angles, so that the four arms are of equal length, the resulting form is called a cross. This is the simplest geometric form in which the cross exists, but the variations both in structure and detail are so innumerable that a very broad view of the subject has been taken in the examples shown. Crosses are also formed by having two or three crossbars bisected by a vertical member, and in some rare instances these are not always at right angles, so that the definition of the term is quite elastic.

The cross (Latin crux, French croix) appears so extensively as the most important and holiest of symbols that we may well simplify the study of its varied forms by classification into three general historical periods. The first period, including all ancient and pagan uses of the cross, dates from about 4000 years before Christ. The very simplest and crudest forms are to be found in this period. The second, or early Christian era, continuing to about 900 A.D., is marked with many interesting variants; while the third period, the late Middle Ages and period of the Crusades, is notable for many richly decorated variations. The history of the cross has been the subject of some 300 volumes. It is not the province of this brief text to supply any small part of it, but merely to touch upon the general significance of the cross, and to identify some of the individual illustrations shown in the plates.

The cross appears in the most widely separated places and remote corners of the earth. It was used by primitive man as an emblem and reappears in the many civilizations that followed. Whether in China, Egypt, Peru, or Patagonia, its symbolism is always associated with reverence and spiritual power; but its greatest prevalence appears with its adoption by Christianity as the exalted emblem of Life Everlasting.

As a cosmic symbol, the cross represents the four quarters of the earth or universe. It may have been derived originally from two crossed sticks, the figure of a bird in flight, or the human figure with outstretched arms. Its ancient source is pure conjecture—we only know it has always meant life. To the ancient Chinese the cross within a square formed the symbol for an enclosed space of earth, and the simple cross occurs as a sign for earth in certain ideographic groups. This device is handed down to us in many ways and appears on many real estate documents today. Also, as an indicator at crossroads, the traveler is familiar with the cross in signposts and railroad warnings. The illiterate, to this day, uses the cross to indicate his signature.

The ancient Tau Cross, an alphabetical sign, is explained by its resemblance to the Key of Life or Crux Ansata, known popularly as the Egyptian Cross. On all sculptures and reliefs, this sign invariably accompanies the Egyptian deities, and on tombs and sarcophagi it signified the immortality of the soul. The Tau Cross, among the ancient Irish, expressed wisdom, and the Mexicans used it to signify the Tree of Life, and fertility.

The heraldic cross originated during the period of the Crusades, when banners, standards, and shields were richly emblazoned with holy insignia, and accessories. The many variants may first have been born of geometric necessity in the partitioning of the shield, but doubtless this need was strongly associated with the Sacred Cross itself Whatever its history and source, the heraldic cross and its many forms constitute one of the brightest spots in the study of decorative devices.

The following brief notes give the names of most of the illustrations shown in this section.

Plate 96. Figs. 856, 857, Latin Cross, or Crux Immissa.

In heraldry, the Passion Cross. Figs. 858, 859, similar to the Lorraine Cross, inverted. Figs. 861-863, Tau Cross, St. Anthony's or Egyptian Cross. Crux Commissa (in Roman times).

Plate 97. Figs. 864-866, Patriarchal Cross. Figs. 867, 868, the eight-ended cross of the Russian Orthodox Church. Fig. 870, Papal Cross, or Triple Cross of the Western peoples. Figs. 869, 871-873, Greek Cross, or Crux Immissa Quadrata, its four arms being of equal length.

Plate 98. These figures are taken from Japanese heraldry. The cross within a circle. Figs. 874-877, 879, and 881, are intended as a sign of the earth quartering in four directions. It is also the character denoting ten.

Plate 99. Figs. 883-891 are variants of the Cross Saltire, or St. Andrew's Cross, named after the patron saint of Scotland. Also called Crux Decussata. When the form appears, as in Figs. 886 and 887, it is called the Cross Voided; when, as in Figs. 888 and 890, it is called the Cross Interlaced.

Plate 100. Figs. 892 and 893, the Cross Potent, or Jerusalem Cross, formed of four Tau Crosses joined. Figs. 894, 895, variations of the foregoing, taken from Japanese heraldry. Figs. 897-900, Cross Crosslet, or Holy Cross; also called German Cross. Fig. 896, Cross Crosslet Saltire, or St. Julian's Cross.

Plate 101. Figs. 901, 902, Cross Degraded. Fig. 903, Cross Degraded, Quarterly-pierced. The latter phrase may be applied to any form of the cross with a square hole the full width of the arms at their intersection. Fig. 904. Cross Potent Quadrate, or St. Chad's Cross. Fig. 905, Crusader's Cross Saltire. Fig. 906, Crusader's Cross, or Jerusalem Cross—also called Cross Cantonnée, which phrase designates any large cross closely surrounded by four smaller ones of similar design. Figs. 907, 908, Cross Potent as central unit, Cantonnée. Fig. 909, Cross Potent Voided.

Plate 102. Figs. 910, 912, Cross Double-Fitchee. Figs. 911, 915, Cross Double-Fitchée Voided. Figs. 913, 914, 916, 917, Cross Aiguisée.

Plate 103. Figs. 919, 920, 921, Maltese Cross variants. Also called Cross of Eight Points. Figs. 922, 923, Cross Patée. Fig. 924, Maltese Cross, the indented ends representing a heraldic version. Figs. 925, 926, Cross Patée Convex. Fig. 927, Cross Patée Convex Voided.

Plate 104. Figs. 928, 930, Cross Patonce. Fig. 929, Cross Fusilée. Figs. 931, 932, Cross Fusilée Voided. Figs. 933, 934, Cross Barbée. Fig. 936, Cross Barbée Voided.

Plate 105. Fig. 937, Cross Patée. Figs. 938, 942, Cross Patonce Voided. Fig. 939, Cross Vair. Figs. 940, 941, Cross Patée Fitchée. Figs. 943-945, Cross Fleurée.

Plate 106. Figs. 946, 947, Cross Moline. Fig. 948, Cross Moline Voided. Fig. 949, Cross Pommée. Fig. 951, Cross Pommée Voided. Figs. 952, 954, Cross Bottonnée, or Cross Tréfflée. Fig. 953, Cross Recercelée.

Plate 107. Fig. 955, Cross Cercelée. Figs. 958, 959, Cross Fourchée. Figs. 960, 963, Cross Millrine. Fig. 962, Cross Potent Convex.

Plate 108. Figs. 964, 966, Interlaced Cross. Figs. 965, 967, Cross Voided. Figs. 968, 969, Triparted Cross. Fig. 970, Cross Wavy Voided.

Plates 109 and 110. Miscellaneous forms. Figs. 974-984 derived from Japanese heraldry. Fig. 985, 986, Cross of Four Fusils, or elongated lozenges. Figs. 988, 990, Cross Demi-sarcelled. Fig. 989, Cross Bezant.

Plate 111. Figs. 992, 993, Cross Lambeau. Figs. 994, 996, Celtic Cross, Irish Cross, or Cross of Iona. Fig. 995, a device resulting from the double crosses, Greek Cross and Cross of St. Andrews, superimposed. Figs. 997, 998, The Double Cross, or Chrismon.

Plates 112 and 113. Figs. 1000, 1001, Egyptian Cross, or Crux Ansata. Figs. 1002-1008, variants of the ancient Anchor Cross. Fig. 1012, Cross Entrailed. Figs. 1016, 1017, Cross Cramponée. Similar to the swastika, except the arms are shorter.

The Four-pointed Star. Plates 114 and 115. The four-pointed star, or Cross Etoile, is the simplest of the stellar variants. It is bi-axial in construction, and, like the cross, is capable of innumerable variations. Fig. 1018 is the simplest of the variants shown, and it is easy to see why the four-pointed star is generally used to indicate the points of the compass.

The Swastika. Plates 116-120. The swastika is generally considered a form of the cross whose extremities are bent back at right angles. This popular device is known by many names, probably because of its widespread distribution throughout the ancient world. From the Sanskrit word, it may be freely translated into "it is well" or "so be it," implying acceptance and denoting life, movement, pleasure, happiness, and good luck. The Anglo-Saxon name is fylfot, from "fower-fot," or "four or many-footed cross." It is also called the gammadion, and Crux Gammata, owing to its being composed of four Greek gammas. The word tetraskele refers to a particular rounded form, Figs. 1063, 1065. In heraldry the swastika is variously known as "Croix Gammée" and "Croix Cramponnée." Theories and speculation as to the origin of the swastika are conflicting. To trace its checkered career would involve a geographical and historical survey of the many countries of the world. This mystic symbol, common to both eastern and western peoples, seems to appear and reappear consistently, yet always is its significance one of happy omen. Reverenced in India some 3000 years before Christ, as a charm against evil, its influence has lasted to this day. In China it has meant perfection, infinity, many blessings. In Japan, where it is called the manji, it represents the number ten thousand, which symbolizes that which is infinite, perfect, and excellent. It is employed as a sign of felicity. It has been found in Persia, Italy, Greece, Cyprus, England, France, and Scandinavia. In America it is found in prehistoric burial grounds in such distantly separated lands as Mexico, Yucatan, Paraguay, and the United States. From the earliest times this famous sign undoubtedly indicated the rotation of the heavens, expressed the power of the sun gods, sky gods, and rain gods, and symbolized all harmonious movement springing from a central source. It is not unreasonable to imagine it as an early ideograph of the sun's disk as a circle with axial motion achieved by the direction of the arms, Fig. 1058. Thus it indicated the daily movement of the sun, and perhaps also the annual change of the seasons.

The many interpretations assigned to the swastika are indeed bewildering. The scholar may trace its history in order to comprehend the power of ancient symbolism. But for the sake of brevity we may conclude by saying that in modern times it is best known as a symbol of motion, good fortune, health, and long life.

Plate 119. Figs. 1066 and 1068 show a device consisting of two facing swastikas. Note the Latin Cross formed in the central axis. Figs. 1069 and 1071, consisting of four swastika forms joined around a central square, are interesting for the complex axial motion produced.

The Pentagon. Plate 121. The pentagon is a plane figure having five equal sides and angles. It is not so frequently used in design as the even-numbered polygons because of the difficulty of construction. However, owing to the prevalence of five-pointed forms in nature, it has served as the basis for a number of designs.

The Five-pointed Star. Plate 122. The five-pointed star is a regular plane figure, formed by joining the alternate points of five points placed at equal distances on the circumference of a circle. As a continuous interlacement, shown in Fig. 1091, it is called the pentacle, or pentagram, and becomes an important element in the history of magic and witchcraft, with many mystic interpretations. It is an ingenious development used in ancient times by the Pythagoreans and others as the pentalpha, an emblem of perfection. This sign was also regarded as a protective fetish, and was frequently worn as an amulet.

The Hexagon. Plates 123-130. The hexagon is a plane, geometric figure, containing six equal sides and angles. It is important because of its occurrence in nature, manifested by the honeycomb, mineral crystals and snow crystals, and its consequent preponderance in design.

By a combination of pure, hexagonal units, as in Plates 125-127, one can see the limitless possibilities of allover patterns that can be produced. In Fig. 1118 an overlapping or interlacing of hexagons produces a supplementary hexagon, whereas in Figs. 1120 and 1121 overlapping results in diamond forms. Figs. 1122-1125 follow the principle of honeycomb structure. Figs. 1126, 1128, and 1131—each consists of three interlaced hexagonal forms, but the resultant designs possess marked variations.

Plate 127, Figs. 1135 and 1143, show clearly that three component elements are generally recognizable in designs whose bases are hexagonal combinations: the hexagon, the six-pointed star, and the diamond. On Plates 128-130 a number of designs are shown whose relationship to the hexagon is easy to see. These are either hexagonal in their enclosing form (Figs. 1144-1149) or those whose sides are varied from the simplicity of the pure hexagon. These designs have been classified as hexagonal variants, as differentiated from a group, subsequently shown, called hex-axial variants.

The Six-pointed Star. Plates 131-133. The six-pointed star is a regular, plane figure formed by joining the alternate points of six points equally spaced on the circumference of a circle. It may also be derived as the result of superimposing two equal-sized equilateral triangles with apices respectively pointing upwards and downwards. According to definition, Figs. 1173, 1174, and 1176 will be the resulting form. The more pointed stellar forms, Figs. 1171 and 1172, satisfy the general conception of a star since they give more of the true, characteristic sparkle associated with the celestial star. Besides its occurrence in many celestial and crystalline forms, the six-pointed star and shape may be abundantly found in the flower world.

The Seal of Solomon. Plate 134. This special form of the six-pointed star, also called the hexagram, is especially interesting both from a structural and symbolical viewpoint. It is formed by the interlacing of two equilateral triangles. In ancient times Solomon is said to have worked many miracles with the aid of this device and hence it has been adopted as the most sacred symbol of the Hebrew race who refer to it by the name, Star of David. This figure represented an ancient notion of deity, since it combined the triangle with apex upward, typifying the masculine, and the triangle with apex downward, the feminine principle.

The Hex-axial Variant. Plates 135-138. This group may logically be considered a further development of the hexagonal variant. However, as the forms become more complex they begin to resemble the snow-crystal and consequently lose their original simplicity and purity of form. The author has called these variants hex-axial because of their construction upon a radial plan of six axes. In the construction of the hex-axial variant it will be seen that the central element is generally a six-pointed star or a hexagon. On Plate 138 the forms shown contain but a few suggestions of the infinity of design based upon radial flower forms. However, this type of design has not been detailed further, since the subject would involve organic forms beyond the scope of this volume.

The Snow-crystal. Plates 139-147. The snow-crystal, one of the most popularly known of all natural motifs, and one of the most exciting demonstrations of the universal laws of geometry, has been highly useful as a source of design. Two essential forms are the elements of which all crystals are formed: fasces of slender, needle-like particles and thin hexagonal plates. There is, generally, greater variety in the interior construction than in the perfect, simple, geometric arrangements of the exterior descent to earth as the forces of cohesion, adhesion, gravity, and temperature act upon the six radii and change their resultant forms. The vast infinity of designs which are revealed by a minute study of these crystalline details forms one of the most fascinating experiences any designer can discover in the entire realm of nature.

The plates of snow-crystals have been arranged in pairs so that each design is shown in both negative and positive forms. Close observation of the two counterparts should reveal valuable points of study.

The Octagon. Plates 148-151. The octagon is a plane, geometric figure containing eight equal sides and angles. Of the many-sided polygons, it is next to the hexagon in importance. Polygons of odd numbered sides, like the heptagon, seven-sided, and nonagon, nine-sided, are seldom used in design, and so have been omitted from this volume.

On Plates 150 and 151 various designs are shown whose bases are either octagonal, or along an eight-axial plan. Fig. 1349 is formed by two squares of equal size superimposed diagonally upon one another. The result, an eight-pointed star, bears a relation in construction to Solomon's Seal, consisting of two superimposed triangles. Fig. 1355 is a device called the octagram, and is formed by a continuous pen stroke describing an eight-pointed star. Fig. 1354 is an ancient classic form of eight radii enclosed within a square, while Fig. 1356 is a variant in which alternate radii have been extended to form an eight-pointed star.

The Eight-pointed Star. Plate 152. Here are shown a number of eight-pointed stars and also stars of a greater number of points. Fig. 1364, formed by the interlacement of two four-pointed stars, is also called an octagram. On Plates 153-155 are shown a number of designs related by their radial construction. Those star-like in character, as in Figs. 1369-1377, have been called stellar variants. Most of these contain twelve points and are derived from Arabian sources where these devices are widely used. These designs, radiating from a circular center, employing either bands or spurs, have been called solar variants. Designs on Plate 154 are derived from Japanese heraldry. Fig. 1388, a device whose rays are wavy, is known in heraldry as an étoile. It is frequently shown with a sun in its center, and as such is called "sun in splendor." Designs on Plate 155 show conclusively that the greater the number of rays, the more dazzling is the solar effect produced.

The Scroll. Plates 156-159 and 163. The most elemental of the many curvilinear motifs is shown in various combinations on Plates 156 and 157. It is basically a C curve or arc of a circle or ellipse whose ends are turned inwardly to form a terminal blob. The examples shown, Figs. 1399-1413, are derived from Japanese heraldry. Plate 158 shows a group of curvilinear motifs, each based upon a triple curve with terminal blobs. These forms are related to the quatrefoil shown on Plate 24. Plates 159 and 163 show additional combinations and designs of curvilinear forms, all based upon Japanese family crests.

The Spiral Scroll and S-scroll. Plates 160 and 161. The spiral is a plane curve describing several or more revolutions around a fixed point, its distance from this point becoming greater at each revolution. It is also called the evolute-spiral and volute. The latter term is more usual in architecture, specifically in such spiral forms as identify the Ionic capital. When the spiral contains a great number of revolutions it is called a whorl. Many ancient forms of the whorl resemble concentric circles and are a decadent and false form of the spiral. A curve whose both ends consist of spirals diametrically opposed in direction, as in Figs. 1435-1437, is called an S-scroll, or S-spiral scroll. A scroll consisting of a slight undulate curve, Figs. 1438 and 1439, is also called an S-scroll. In architecture this undulate curve is called an ogee, or, as applied to moulding forms, a cyma recta or cyma reversa, depending upon the position of alternate curves. Plate 161 shows pairs and groups of spiral forms, and it is easy to see how important and useful these motifs become in the field of decoration. The origins and history of the spiral have been the subject of much conjecture, but it is clear that its frequency in nature has had much influence on its adoption by many savage and primitive peoples, and its subsequent development. Whether the spiral is of animistic or technomorphic origin, whether it was of flexible vegetable origin before it became formalized, or whether it was first inspired by familiar marine forms, will remain an open question. The ram's horn, the nautilus shell, the spiral nebulae, and the vine tendril are but a few of the most common occurrences of the spiral in nature. The spiral has little symbolical interpretation, but in the East the spiral denotes thunder from which issues a flash of lightning.

The Triskelion and Tetraskelion. Plates 162 and 165. The triskelion is a tri-radial figure whose three arms may be simple curves, scrolls, or angular lines. The tetraskelion consists of four arms, and is similar to the swastika. The triskelion is of ancient origin and has been found to exist in many variants. In its earliest appearance the triskelion is a simple geometrical figure, but later the three radial elements become revolving legs and, in still another Roman version, they develop into dragon's heads. It appears on the coins of ancient Lycia and, later, as the three-pointed symbol of the land of Trinakria, i.e., the "Three Capes," the ancient name of Sicily. Figs. 1477, 1478, 1480, and 1481 are forms in which volutes conjoin with one another to produce interesting variants.

The Wave Scroll. Plate 164. The wave scroll, or evolute scroll, also called by the ancient Greeks the Vitruvian scroll, is a special form of the scroll previously observed in Plates 156-159. It generally takes the form of a border, or succession of curves each being terminated at one end by a volute from which the next curve springs. When scrolls from opposite directions meet at a central point, the two central scrolls unite to produce forms as in Figs. 1471 and 1473.

The Monad. Plate 166. The monad is a plane, geometric figure of a circle divided by two equal tangential arcs with opposite centers. Fig. 1486 is its most familiar form, being the two comma-shaped halves usually contrasted in black and white. This device (variously called "yang and yin" in Chinese, "futatsu tomoe" in Japanese, "tah-gook" in Korean) is one of the most familiar figures in Japanese and Chinese art, and finds wide application in the decorative arts.

Notes on the Plates 215

The Chinese diagram, yang and yin, represents the dual principles in nature: yang—bright, yin—dark; yang—the principle of heaven, yin—the earth; yang is the sun, yin, the moon; yang is the active, masculine principle, yin, the passive, feminine principle; yang is positive, yin, negative.

The Triad. Plate 167. The three-comma-shaped figure, called in Japanese "mitsu tomoe," is shown in Figs. 1492 and 1494-1497. It expresses the universal idea of trinity and bears some similarity to the triskelion, or "three-legged symbol," previously noted. The forms shown are derived from Japanese family crests.

The Circular Enclosure. Plates 168 and 169. Here are shown a few simple types of circular design upon which ornament may be further developed. Figs. 1504 and 1506 show concentric or zonal subdivisions. Figs. 1505, 1507, and 1509 show rectangular and interlocking units. In Figs. 1508, 1510, and 1512, radial divisions are indicated. The undulating curve is noted in Fig. 1511, and designs based upon it in Figs. 1516, 1518, and 1519. The skirl, or whirling curvilinear motif, Figs. 1513-1515, produces a restless, rotary motion. Fig. 1517 shows the circular wave band. Figs. 1520, 1521, and 1522-1525, continuing on Plate 170, are familiar Oriental forms of the curvilinear enclosure.

The Loop and Guilloche. Plate 172. The loop is the simplest form of the twist or interlacement, and consists of a continuous line forming a figure eight. The guilloche is a full-rounded circular form of the loop, and is usually employed in continuous border patterns. It is common to many ancient art cultures, especially the Egyptian, Assyrian, and Roman, and is probably of technomorphic origin. Fig. 1541 is the mathematical sign of infinity.

The Curvilinear Interlacement, etc. Plates 173 and 176. The triple-looped interlacement, similar in construction to the triquetra (Plate 64), except that its ends are rounded. The four-looped interlacements, Figs. 1552 and 1554, and the quatrefoil, Fig. 1553, may be considered among the simpler devices upon which an elaborate system of interlacements can be built. Very often curvilinear interlacements will contain pointed or arched members, constructed of segments of circles, as in Figs. 1561-1563. Fig. 1568 is derived from a composite of three triquetrous forms, centrally joined. Figs. 1576 and 1581 are somewhat similar in outward appearance, but the former has a continuous thread of design while the latter consists of three separate quatrefoils interlaced. Interlacements are found in many styles of decoration but in some they become the predominating background, especially in the Celtic and Scandinavian decorative arts.

The Rectangular and Angular Interlacement. Plates 177-179. Of the various forms of interlacements, the rectangular, with its rigidity and formality, appears to a lesser extent than do other forms. As the crossbands become more numerous and the designs more complex, the character of plaiting and weaving from which these motifs undoubtedly spring, is more obvious. Compare Fig. 1607 with 1571, on Plate 175; the former, angular, and the latter, curvilinear, offer counterparts in varied treatment.

The Fret. Plates 180-184. The fret is usually considered in terms of a border or pattern, rarely as an isolated, elemental device as shown here. The fret, or meander (derived from the name of a winding river in Asia Minor, now called Menderes), is a plane, rectangular motif taken from early Greek ornament. It is also, in some instances, known as the key pattern, the simplest forms of which, like Fig. 1623, are reciprocal forms and T-shapes in which the interspaces are of the same character as the solid between them. Fret patterns are the angular or rectangular counterparts of the spiral or wave pattern, noted on Plate 164. The serpentine, or meandering, characteristic may best be observed in Figs. 1614, 1621, 1622, etc. The rectangular variants, Figs. 1618 and 1619, are often associated with the fret, and are interpolated between alternate motifs. On Plate 181, Figs. 1624-1626 are of Japanese origin, the remainder, Greek. Fig. 1635 is the corner motif corresponding to Fig. 1634. Fig. 1637, as well as all examples on Plates 183 and 184, are derived from Japanese heraldry. The sharply angular and curvilinear variants are rarely found in Occidental designs.

Plates 184-188. The simple division of the square or rectangle may be achieved in many ways, and is frequently based upon a bi-symmetrical arrangement along the two intersecting diameters, or diagonals. But in the examples shown on Plates 185 and 186 a mon-axial plan has been followed, and a number of variations, not entirely symmetrical, have been given. From these simple variations develop the more complex devices utilizing Japanese characters. All the examples shown are based upon Japanese heraldry.

The Shield and Its Subdivisions. Plates 189-193. In introducing examples of the variant shapes and ordinaries of the shield, no attempt has been made to involve the subject of heraldry in this work, but merely, insofar as these forms may possess names and terms, to utilize the nomenclature of heraldry, wherever possible, to identify them.

The shield is a most important form in heraldry for on it are exhibited the many signs and elements that constitute the complex language of heraldry. The simpler forms of the shield are derived originally from articles of defensive warfare dating back to ancient times, but in later periods a fuller freedom and more artistic imagination accounted for innumerable fantastic shapes. The prevailing styles of architecture and decoration doubtless left their impress, as seen in the rounded and pointed or Gothic arch forms, inverted, of course. Figures on Plate 189 show the half-round forms which first appeared during the Fourteenth Century. Plates 190 and 191 exhibit the pointed form. The oldest shape is the triangular or "heater-shaped" shield, Figs. 1708, 1710, and 1720-1722, used as early as the Twelfth Century. Figs. 1729-1734, Plate 193, show forms popular during the Italian Renaissance. Figs. 1735-1737 display the keystone, so called because it is the central stone in an arched construction.

Plates 194-204. The various subdivisions of the shield produce geometrical figures called, in heraldry, the ordinaries. The shield is divided into different fields by the use of straight or curved lines extended to the margins of the shield. Very often the lines used for these divisions take on decorative form, such as the wavy and zigzag lines, and many others, called lines of partition. A description of the figures, or blazoning, gives the heraldic terms. For further detailed study of these forms, it is suggested that books on heraldry listed in the bibliography, be consulted.

Dover Books on Art

THE FOUR BOOKS OF ARCHITECTURE, Andrea Palladio. A compendium of the art of Andrea Palladio, one of the most celebrated architects of the Renaissance, including 250 magnificently-engraved plates showing edifices either of Palladio's design or reconstructed (in these drawings) by him from classical ruins and contemporary accounts. 257 plates. xxiv + 119pp. 9½ x 12¾. 21308-0 Clothbound $10.00

150 MASTERPIECES OF DRAWING, A. Toney. Selected by a gifted artist and teacher, these are some of the finest drawings produced by Western artists from the early 15th to the end of the 18th centuries. Excellent reproductions of drawings by Rembrandt, Bruegel, Raphael, Watteau, and other familiar masters, as well as works by lesser known but brilliant artists. 150 plates. xviii + 150pp. 5⅜ x 11¼. 21032-4 Paperbound $2.00

MORE DRAWINGS BY HEINRICH KLEY. Another collection of the graphic, vivid sketches of Heinrich Kley, one of the most diabolically talented cartoonists of our century. The sketches take in every aspect of human life: nothing is too sacred for him to ridicule, no one too eminent for him to satirize. 158 drawings you will not easily forget. iv + 104pp. 7⅜ x 10¾. 20041-8 Paperbound $1.85

THE TRIUMPH OF MAXIMILIAN I, 137 Woodcuts by Hans Burgkmair and Others. This is one of the world's great art monuments, a series of magnificent woodcuts executed by the most important artists in the German realms as part of an elaborate plan by Maximilian I, ruler of the Holy Roman Empire, to commemorate his own name, dynasty, and achievements. 137 plates. New translation of descriptive text, notes, and bibliography prepared by Stanley Appelbaum. Special section of 10pp. containing a reduced version of the entire Triumph. x + 169pp. 11⅛ x 9¼. 21207-6 Paperbound $3.00

LOST EXAMPLES OF COLONIAL ARCHITECTURE, J. M. Howells. This book offers a unique guided tour through America's architectural past, all of which is either no longer in existence or so changed that its original beauty has been destroyed. More than 275 clear photos of old churches, dwelling houses, public buildings, business structures, etc. 245 plates, containing 281 photos and 9 drawings, floorplans, etc. New Index. xvii + 248pp. 7⅞ x 10¾. 21143-6 Paperbound $3.00

AFRICAN SCULPTURE, Ladislas Segy. 163 full-page plates illustrating masks, fertility figures, ceremonial objects, etc., of 50 West and Central African tribes—95% never before illustrated. 34-page introduction to African sculpture. "Mr. Segy is one of its top authorities," NEW YORKER. 164 full-page photographic plates. Introduction. Bibliography. 244pp. 6⅛ x 9¼.

20396-4 Paperbound $2.25

CALLIGRAPHY, J. G. Schwandner. First reprinting in 200 years of this legendary book of beautiful handwriting. Over 300 ornamental initials, 12 complete calligraphic alphabets, over 150 ornate frames and panels, 75 calligraphic pictures of cherubs, stags, lions, etc., thousands of flourishes, scrolls, etc., by the greatest 18th-century masters. All material can be copied or adapted without permission. Historical introduction. 158 full-page plates. 368pp. 9 x 13.

20475-8 Clothbound $10.00

A DIDEROT PICTORIAL ENCYCLOPEDIA OF TRADES AND INDUSTRY. Manufacturing and the Technical Arts in Plates Selected from "L'Encyclopédie ou Dictionnaire Raisonné des Sciences, des Arts, et des Métiers," of Denis Diderot, edited with text by C. Gillispie. Over 2000 illustrations on 485 full-page plates. Magnificent 18th-century engravings of men, women, and children working at such trades as milling flour, cheesemaking, charcoal burning, mining, silverplating, shoeing horses, making fine glass, printing, hundreds more, showing details of machinery, different steps in sequence, etc. A remarkable art work, but also the largest collection of working figures in print, copyright-free, for art directors, designers, etc. Two vols. 920pp. 9 x 12. Heavy library cloth.

22284-5, 22285-3 Two volume set $22.50

SILK SCREEN TECHNIQUES, J. Biegeleisen, M. Cohn. A practical step-by-step home course in one of the most versatile, least expensive graphic arts processes. How to build an inexpensive silk screen, prepare stencils, print, achieve special textures, use color, etc. Every step explained, diagrammed. 149 illustrations, 201pp. 6⅛ x 9¼.

20433-2 Paperbound $2.00

STICKS AND STONES, Lewis Mumford. An examination of forces influencing American architecture: the medieval tradition in early New England, the classical influence in Jefferson's time, the Brown Decades, the imperial facade, the machine age, etc. "A truly remarkable book," SAT. REV. OF LITERATURE. 2nd revised edition. 21 illus. xvii + 240pp. 5⅜ x 8.

20202-X Paperbound $2.00

Dover Books on Art

STYLES IN PAINTING, Paul Zucker. By comparing paintings of similar subject matter, the author shows the characteristics of various painting styles. You are shown at a glance the differences between reclining nudes by Giorgione, Velasquez, Goya, Modigliani; how a Byzantine portrait is unlike a portrait by Van Eyck, da Vinci, Dürer, or Marc Chagall; how the painting of landscapes has changed gradually from ancient Pompeii to Lyonel Feininger in our own century. 241 beautiful, sharp photographs illustrate the text. xiv + 338 pp. $5\frac{5}{8}$ x $8\frac{1}{4}$.
20760-9 Paperbound $2.25

THE PRACTICE OF TEMPERA PAINTING, D. V. Thompson, Jr. Used in Egyptian and Minoan wall paintings and in much of the fine work of Giotto, Botticelli, Titian, and many others, tempera has long been regarded as one of the finest painting methods known. This is the definitive work on the subject by the world's outstanding authority. He covers the uses and limitations of tempera, designing, drawing with the brush, incising outlines, applying to metal, mixing and preserving tempera, varnishing and guilding, etc. Appendix, "Tempera Practice in Yale Art School" by Prof. L. E. York. 4 full page plates. 85 illustrations. x + 141pp. $5\frac{3}{8}$ x $8\frac{1}{2}$.   20343-3 Paperbound $1.75

GRAPHIC WORLDS OF PETER BRUEGEL THE ELDER, H. A. Klein. 64 of the finest etchings and engravings made from the drawings of the Flemish master Peter Bruegel. Every aspect of the artist's diversified style and subject matter is represented, with notes providing biographical and other background information. Excellent reproductions on opaque stock with nothing on reverse side. 63 engravings, 1 woodcut. Bibliography. xviii + 289pp. $11\frac{3}{8}$ x $8\frac{1}{4}$.   21132-0 Paperbound $3.50

A HISTORY OF ENGRAVING AND ETCHING, A. M. Hind. Beginning with the anonymous masters of 15th century engraving, this highly regarded and thorough survey carries you through Italy, Holland, and Germany to the great engravers and beginnings of etching in the 16th century, through the portrait engravers, master etchers, practicioners of mezzotint, crayon manner and stipple, aquatint, color prints, to modern etching in the period just prior to World War I. Beautifully illustrated —sharp clear prints on heavy opaque paper. Author's preface. 3 appendixes. 111 illustrations. xviii + 487 pp. $5\frac{3}{8}$ x $8\frac{1}{2}$.
20954-7 Paperbound $3.00

FOOT-HIGH LETTERS: A GUIDE TO LETTERING, M. Price.
28 15½ x 22½″ plates, give classic Roman alphabet, one foot
high per letter, plus 9 other 2″ high letter forms for each letter.
16 page syllabus. Ideal for lettering classes, home study. 28 plates
in box.   20239-9 $600

A HANDBOOK OF WEAVES, G. H. Oelsner. Most complete
book of weaves, fully explained, differentiated, illustrated. Plain
weaves, irregular, double-stitched, filling satins; derivative,
basket, rib weaves; steep, broken, herringbone, twills, lace, tricot,
many others. Translated, revised by S. S. Dale; supplement on
analysis of weaves. Bible for all handweavers. 1875 illustrations.
410pp. 6⅛ x 9¼.   20209-7 Clothbound $7.50

*JAPANESE HOMES AND THEIR SURROUNDINGS, E. S.
Morse.* Classic describes, analyses, illustrates all aspects of traditional Japanese home, from plan and structure to appoint-
ments, furniture, etc. Published in 1886, before Japanese architecture was contaminated by Western, this is strikingly modern
in beautiful, functional approach to living. Indispensable to every
architect, interior decorator, designer. 307 illustrations. Glossary.
410pp. 5⅝ x 8⅜.   20746-3 Paperbound $2.50

THE DRAWINGS OF HEINRICH KLEY. Uncut publication of
long-sought-after sketchbooks of satiric, ironic iconoclast. Remarkable fantasy, weird symbolism, brilliant technique make
Kley a shocking experience to layman, endless source of ideas,
techniques for artist. 200 drawings, original size, captions translated. Introduction. 136pp. 6 x 9.   20024-8 Paperbound $2.00

COSTUMES OF THE ANCIENTS, Thomas Hope. Beautiful,
clear, sharp line drawings of Greek and Roman figures in full
costume, by noted artist and antiquary of early 19th century.
Dress, armor, divinities, masks, etc. Invaluable sourcebook for
costumers, designers, first-rate picture file for illustrators, commercial artists. Introductory text by Hope. 300 plates. 6 x 9.
                                                   20021-3 Paperbound $2.00

VITRUVIUS: TEN BOOKS ON ARCHITECTURE. The most
influential book in the history of architecture. 1st century A.D.
Roman classic has influenced such men as Bramante, Palladio,
Michelangelo, up to present. Classic principles of design, har-
mony, etc. Fascinating reading. Definitive English translation by
Professor H. Morgan, Harvard. 344pp. 5⅜ x 8.
                                                   20645-9 Paperbound $2.50

GREEK REVIVAL ARCHITECTURE IN AMERICA, T. Hamlin. A comprehensive study of the American Classical Revival, its regional variations, reasons for its success and eventual decline. Profusely illustrated with photos, sketches, floor plans and sections, displaying the work of almost every important architect of the time. 2 appendices. 39 figures, 94 plates containing 221 photos, 62 architectural designs, drawings, etc. 324-item classified bibliography. Index. xi + 439pp. 5⅜ x 8½.
21148-7 Paperbound $3.50

CREATIVE LITHOGRAPHY AND HOW TO DO IT, Grant Arnold. Written by a man who practiced and taught lithography for many years, this highly useful volume explains all the steps of the lithographic process from tracing the drawings on the stone to printing the lithograph, with helpful hints for solving special problems. Index. 16 reproductions of lithographs. 11 drawings. xv + 214pp. of text. 5⅜ x 8½.
21208-4 Paperbound $2.25

TEACH YOURSELF ANTIQUE COLLECTING, E. Bradford. An excellent, brief guide to collecting British furniture, silver, pictures and prints, pewter, pottery and porcelain, Victoriana, enamels, clocks or other antiques. Much background information difficult to find elsewhere. 15pp. of illus. 215pp. 7 x 4¼.
21368-4 Clothbound $2.00

THE STANDARD BOOK OF QUILT MAKING AND COLLECTING, M. Ickis. Even if you are a beginner, you will soon find yourself quilting like an expert, by following these clearly drawn patterns, photographs, and step-by-step instructions. Learn how to plan the quilt, to select the pattern to harmonize with the design and color of the room, to choose materials. Over 40 full-size patterns. Index. 483 illustrations. One color plate. xi + 276pp. 6¾ x 9½.   20582-7 Paperbound $2.50

THE ENJOYMENT AND USE OF COLOR, W. Sargent. Requiring no special technical know-how, this book tells you all about color and how it is created, perceived, and imitated in art. Covers many little-known facts about color values, intensities, effects of high and low illumination, complementary colors, and color harmonies. Simple do-it-yourself experiments and observations. 35 illustrations, including 6 full-page color plates. New color frontispiece. Index. x + 274 pp. 5⅜ x 8.
20944-X Paperbound $2.25

HANDBOOK OF DESIGNS AND DEVICES, C. P. Hornung. A remarkable working collection of 1836 basic designs and variations, all copyright-free. Variations of circle, line, cross, diamond, swastika, star, scroll, shield, many more. Notes on symbolism. "A necessity to every designer who would be original without having to labor heavily," ARTIST AND ADVERTISER. 204 plates. 240pp. 5⅜ x 8. 20125-2 Paperbound $2.00

THE UNIVERSAL PENMAN, George Bickham. Exact reproduction of beautiful 18th-century book of handwriting. 22 complete alphabets in finest English roundhand, other scripts, over 2000 elaborate flourishes, 122 calligraphic illustrations, etc. Material is copyright-free. "An essential part of any art library, and a book of permanent value," AMERICAN ARTIST. 212 plates. 224pp. 9 x 13¾. 20020-5 Clothbound $12.50

AN ATLAS OF ANATOMY FOR ARTISTS, F. Schider. This standard work contains 189 full-page plates, more than 647 illustrations of all aspects of the human skeleton, musculature, cutaway portions of the body, each part of the anatomy, hand forms, eyelids, breasts, location of muscles under the flesh, etc. 59 plates illustrate how Michelangelo, da Vinci, Goya, 15 others, drew human anatomy. New 3rd edition enlarged by 52 new illustrations by Cloquet, Barcsay. "The standard reference tool," AMERICAN LIBRARY ASSOCIATION. "Excellent," AMERICAN ARTIST. 189 plates, 647 illustrations. xxvi + 192pp. 7⅞ x 10⅝. 20241-0 Clothbound $6.50

AN ATLAS OF ANIMAL ANATOMY FOR ARTISTS, W. Ellenberger, H. Baum, H. Dittrich. The largest, richest animal anatomy for artists in English. Form, musculature, tendons, bone structure, expression, detailed cross sections of head, other features, of the horse, lion, dog, cat, deer, seal, kangaroo, cow, bull, goat, monkey, hare, many other animals. "Highly recommended," DESIGN. Second, revised, enlarged edition with new plates from Cuvier, Stubbs, etc. 288 illustrations. 153pp. 11⅜ x 9. 20082-5 Paperbound $2.50

VASARI ON TECHNIQUE, G. Vasari. Pupil of Michelangelo, outstanding biographer of Renaissance artists reveals technical methods of his day. Marble, bronze, fresco painting, mosaics, engraving, stained glass, rustic ware, etc. Only English translation, extensively annotated by G. Baldwin Brown. 18 plates. 342pp. 5⅜ x 8. 20717-X Paperbound $2.75

Dover Books on Art

HAWTHORNE ON PAINTING. Vivid re-creation, from students' notes, of instructions by Charles Hawthorne at Cape Cod School of Art. Essays, epigrammatic comments on color, form, seeing, techniques, etc. "Excellent," Time. 100pp. 5⅜ x 8.

20653-X Paperbound $1.25

THE HANDBOOK OF PLANT AND FLORAL ORNAMENT, R. G. Hatton. 1200 line illustrations, from medieval, Renaissance herbals, of flowering or fruiting plants: garden flowers, wild flowers, medicinal plants, poisons, industrial plants, etc. A unique compilation that probably could not be matched in any library in the world. Formerly"The Craftsman's Plant-Book." Also full text on uses, history as ornament, etc. 548pp. 6⅛ x 9¼.

20649-1 Paperbound $3.50

DECORATIVE ALPHABETS AND INITIALS, Alexander Nesbitt. 91 complete alphabets, over 3900 ornamental initials, from Middle Ages, Renaissance printing, baroque, rococo, and modern sources. Individual items copyright free, for use in commercial art, crafts, design, packaging, etc. 123 full-page plates. 3924 initials. 129pp. 7¾ x 10¾.

20544-4 Paperbound $2.50

METHODS AND MATERIALS OF THE GREAT SCHOOLS AND MASTERS, Sir Charles Eastlake. (Formerly titled "Materials for a History of Oil Painting.") Vast, authentic reconstruction of secret techniques of the masters, recreated from ancient manuscripts, contemporary accounts, analysis of paintings, etc. Oils, fresco, tempera, varnishes, encaustics. Both Flemish and Italian schools, also British and French. One of great works for art historians, critics; inexhaustible mine of suggestions, information for practicing artists. Total of 1025pp. 5⅜ x 8.

20718-8, 20719-6 Two volume set, Paperbound $5.00

BYZANTINE ART AND ARCHAEOLOGY, O. M. Dalton. Still most thorough work in English on Byzantine art forms throughout ancient and medieval world. Analyzes hundreds of pieces, covers sculpture, painting, mosaic, jewelry, textiles, architecture, etc. Historical development; specific examples; iconology and ideas; symbolism. A treasure-trove of material about one of most important art traditions, will supplement and expand any other book in area. Bibliography of over 2500 items. 457 illustrations. 747pp. 6⅛ x 9¼.

20776-5 Clothbound $8.50

LANDSCAPE GARDENING IN JAPAN, Josiah Conder. A detailed picture of Japanese gardening techniques and ideas, the artistic principles incorporated in the Japanese garden, and the religious and ethical concepts at the heart of those principles. Preface. 92 illustrations, plus all 40 full-page plates from the Supplement. Index. xv + 299pp. 8⅜ x 11¼.

21216-5 Paperbound $3.50

DESIGN AND FIGURE CARVING, E. J. Tangerman. "Anyone who can peel a potato can carve," states the author, and in this unusual book he shows you how, covering every stage in detail from very simple exercises working up to museum-quality pieces. Terrific aid for hobbyists, arts and crafts counselors, teachers, those who wish to make reproductions for the commercial market. Appendix: How to Enlarge a Design. Brief bibliography. Index. 1298 figures. x + 289pp. 5⅜ x 8½.

21209-2 Paperbound $2.00

WILD FOWL DECOYS, Joel Barber. Antique dealers, collectors, craftsmen, hunters, readers of Americana, etc. will find this the only thorough and reliable guide on the market today to this unique folk art. It contains the history, cultural significance, regional design variations; unusual decoy lore; working plans for constructing decoys; and loads of illustrations. 140 full-page plates, 4 in color. 14 additional plates of drawings and plans by the author. xxvii + 156pp. 7⅞ x 10¾. 20011-6 Paperbound $3.50

1800 WOODCUTS BY THOMAS BEWICK AND HIS SCHOOL. This is the largest collection of first-rate pictorial woodcuts in print—an indispensable part of the working library of every commercial artist, art director, production designer, packaging artist, craftsman, manufacturer, librarian, art collector, and artist. And best of all, when you buy your copy of Bewick, you buy the rights to reproduce individual illustrations—no permission needed, no acknowledgments, no clearance fees! Classified index. Bibliography and sources. xiv + 246pp. 9 x 12.

20766-8 Paperbound $4.00

THE SCRIPT LETTER, Tommy Thompson. Prepared by a noted authority, this is a thorough, straightforward course of instruction with advice on virtually every facet of the art of script lettering. Also a brief history of lettering with examples from early copy books and illustrations from present day advertising and packaging. Copiously illustrated. Bibliography. 128pp. 6½ x 9⅛.

21311-0 Paperbound $1.25

PRINCIPLES OF ART HISTORY, H. Wölfflin. This remarkably instructive work demonstrates the tremendous change in artistic conception from the 14th to the 18th centuries, by analyzing 164 works by Botticelli, Dürer, Hobbema, Holbein, Hals, Titian, Rembrandt, Vermeer, etc., and pointing out exactly what is meant by "baroque," "classic," "primitive," "picturesque," and other basic terms of art history and criticism. "A remarkable lesson in the art of seeing," SAT. REV. OF LITERATURE. Translated from the 7th German edition. 150 illus. 254pp. 6⅛ x 9¼.   20276-3   Paperbound $2.25

FOUNDATIONS OF MODERN ART, A. Ozenfant. Stimulating discussion of human creativity from paleolithic cave painting to modern painting, architecture, decorative arts. Fully illustrated with works of Gris, Lipchitz, Léger, Picasso, primitive, modern artifacts, architecture, industrial art, much more. 226 illustrations. 368pp. 6⅛ x 9¼.   20215-1   Paperbound $2.50

METALWORK AND ENAMELLING, H. Maryon. Probably the best book ever written on the subject. Tells everything necessary for the home manufacture of jewelry, rings, ear pendants, bowls, etc. Covers materials, tools, soldering, filigree, setting stones, raising patterns, repoussé work, damascening, niello, cloisonné, polishing, assaying, casting, and dozens of other techniques. The best substitute for apprenticeship to a master metalworker. 363 photos and figures. 374pp. 5½ x 8½.
T183   Clothbound $8.50

SHAKER FURNITURE, E. D. and F. Andrews. The most illuminating study of Shaker furniture ever written. Covers chronology, craftsmanship, houses, shops, etc. Includes over 200 photographs of chairs, tables, clocks, beds, benches, etc. "Mr. & Mrs. Andrews know all there is to know about Shaker furniture," Mark Van Doren, NATION. 48 full-page plates. 192pp. 7⅞ x 10¾.   20679-3   Paperbound $2.50

ANIMAL DRAWING: ANATOMY AND ACTION FOR ARTISTS, C. R. Knight. 158 studies, with full accompanying text, of such animals as the gorilla, bear, bison, dromedary, camel, vulture, pelican, iguana, shark, etc., by one of the greatest modern masters of animal drawing. Innumerable tips on how to get life expression into your work. "An excellent reference work," SAN FRANCISCO CHRONICLE. 158 illustrations. 156pp. 10½ x 8½.   20426-X   Paperbound $2.75

MASTERPIECES OF FURNITURE, Verna Cook Salomonsky. Photographs and measured drawings of some of the finest examples of Colonial American, 17th century English, Windsor, Sheraton, Hepplewhite, Chippendale, Louis XIV, Queen Anne, and various other furniture styles. The textual matter includes information on traditions, characteristics, background, etc. of various pieces. 101 plates. Bibliography. 224pp. 7⅞ x 10¾.

21381-1 Paperbound $2.50

PRIMITIVE ART, Franz Boas. In this exhaustive volume, a great American anthropologist analyzes all the fundamental traits of primitive art, covering the formal element in art, representative art, symbolism, style, literature, music, and the dance. Illustrations of Indian embroidery, paleolithic paintings, woven blankets, wing and tail designs, totem poles, cutlery, earthenware, baskets and many other primitive objects and motifs. Over 900 illustrations. 376pp. 5⅜ x 8.   20025-6 Paperbound $2.50

AN INTRODUCTION TO A HISTORY OF WOODCUT, A. M. Hind. Nearly all of this authoritative 2-volume set is devoted to the 15th century—the period during which the woodcut came of age as an important art form. It is the most complete compendium of information on this period, the artists who contributed to it, and their technical and artistic accomplishments. Profusely illustrated with cuts by 15th century masters, and later works for comparative purposes. 484 illustrations. 5 indexes. Total of xi + 838pp. 5⅜ x 8½. Two-vols. 20952-0, 20953-9 Paperbound $5.50

ART STUDENTS' ANATOMY, E. J. Farris. Teaching anatomy by using chiefly living objects for illustration, this study has enjoyed long popularity and success in art courses and home-study programs. All the basic elements of the human anatomy are illustrated in minute detail, diagrammed and pictured as they pass through common movements and actions. 158 drawings, photographs, and roentgenograms. Glossary of anatomical terms. x + 159pp. 5⅝ x 8⅜.   20744-7 Paperbound $1.50

COLONIAL LIGHTING, A. H. Hayward. The only book to cover the fascinating story of lamps and other lighting devices in America. Beginning with rush light holders used by the early settlers, it ranges through the elaborate chandeliers of the Federal period, illustrating 647 lamps. Of great value to antique collectors, designers, and historians of arts and crafts. Revised and enlarged by James R. Marsh. xxxi + 198pp. 5⅝ x 8¼.

20975-X Paperbound $2.00

Dover Books on Art

ARCHITECTURAL AND PERSPECTIVE DESIGNS, Giuseppe Galli Bibiena. 50 imaginative scenic drawings of Giuseppe Galli Bibiena, principal theatrical engineer and architect to the Viennese court of Charles VI. Aside from its interest to art historians, students, and art lovers, there is a whole Baroque world of material in this book for the commercial artist. Portrait of Charles VI by Martin de Meytens. 1 allegorical plate. 50 additional plates. New introduction. vi + 103pp. 10⅛ x 13¼.
21263-7 Paperbound $2.50

PRINTED EPHEMERA, edited and collected by John Lewis. This book contains centuries of design, typographical and pictorial motives in proven, effective commercial layouts. Hundreds of the most striking examples of labels, tickets, posters, wrappers, programs, menus, and other items have been collected in this handsome and useful volume, along with information on the dimensions and colors of the original, printing processes used, stylistic notes on typography and design, etc. Study this book and see how the best commercial artists of the past and present have solved their particular problems. Most of the material is copyright free. 713 illustrations, many in color. Illustrated index of type faces included. Glossary of technical terms. Indexes. 288pp. 9¼ x 12.
21037-5 Clothbound $15.00

DESIGN FOR ARTISTS AND CRAFTSMEN, Louis Wolchonok. Recommended for either individual or classroom use, this book helps you to create original designs from things about you, from geometric patterns, from plants, animals, birds, humans, landscapes, manmade objects. "A great contribution," N. Y. Society of Craftsmen. 113 exercises with hints and diagrams. More than 1280 illustrations. xv + 207pp. 7⅞ x 10¾.
20274-7 Paperbound $2.75

ART AND THE SOCIAL ORDER, D. W. Gotshalk. Is art only an extension of society? Is it completely isolated? In this delightfully written book, Professor Gotshalk supplies some workable answers. He discusses various theories of art from Plato to Marx and Freud and uses all areas of visual arts, music and literature to elaborate his views. "Seems to me the soundest and most penetrating work on the philosophy of art to appear in recent years," C. J. Ducasse, Brown Univ. Addenda: "Postscript to Chapter X: 1962." Bibliography in notes. Index. xviii + 255pp. 5⅜ x 8½.
20294-1 Paperbound $1.75

200 DECORATIVE TITLE-PAGES, edited by A. Nesbitt. Fascinating and informative from a historical point of view, this beautiful collection of decorated titles will be a great inspiration to students of design, commercial artists, advertising designers, etc. A complete survey of the genre from the first known decorated title to work in the first decades of this century. Bibliography and sources of the plates. 222pp. 8⅜ x 11¼.

21264-5 Paperbound $2.75

ON THE LAWS OF JAPANESE PAINTING, H. P. Bowie. This classic work on the philosophy and technique of Japanese art is based on the author's first-hand experiences studying art in Japan. Every aspect of Japanese painting is described: the use of the brush and other materials; laws governing conception and execution; subjects for Japanese paintings, etc. The best possible substitute for a series of lessons from a great Oriental master. Index. xv + 117pp. + 66 plates. 6⅛ x 9¼.

20030-2 Paperbound $2.25

PAINTING IN THE FAR EAST, L. Binyon. A study of over 1500 years of Oriental art by one of the world's outstanding authorities. The author chooses the most important masters in each period—Wu Tao-tzu, Toba Sojo, Kanaoka, Li Lung-mien, Masanobu, Okio, etc.—and examines the works, schools, and influence of each within their cultural context. 42 photographs. Sources of original works and selected bibliography. Notes including list of principal painters by periods. xx + 297pp. 6⅛ x 9¼.

20520-7 Paperbound $2.50

THE ALPHABET AND ELEMENTS OF LETTERING, F. W. Goudy. A beautifully illustrated volume on the aesthetics of letters and type faces and their history and development. Each plate consists of 15 forms of a single letter with the last plate devoted to the ampersand and the numerals. "A sound guide for all persons engaged in printing or drawing," Saturday Review. 27 full-page plates. 48 additional figures. xii + 131pp. 7⅞ x 10¾.

20792-7 Paperbound $2.25

PAINTING IN ISLAM, Sir Thomas W. Arnold. This scholarly study puts Islamic painting in its social and religious context and examines its relation to Islamic civilization in general. 65 full-page plates illustrate the text and give outstanding examples of Islamic art. 4 appendices. Index of mss. referred to. General Index. xxiv + 159pp. 6⅝ x 9¼.   21310-2 Paperbound $2.75

Dover Books on Art

THE COMPLETE BOOK OF SILK SCREEN PRINTING PRO-DUCTION, J. I. Biegeleisen. Here is a clear and complete picture of every aspect of silk screen technique and press operation—from individually operated manual presses to modern automatic ones. Unsurpassed as a guidebook for setting up shop, making shop operation more efficient, finding out about latest methods and equipment; or as a textbook for use in teaching, studying, or learning all aspects of the profession. 124 figures. Index. Bibliography. List of Supply Sources. xi + 253pp. 5⅜ x 8½.

21100-2 Paperbound $2.75

A HISTORY OF COSTUME, Carl Köhler. The most reliable and authentic account of the development of dress from ancient times through the 19th century. Based on actual pieces of clothing that have survived, using paintings, statues and other reproductions only where originals no longer exist. Hundreds of illustrations, including detailed patterns for many articles. Highly useful for theatre and movie directors, fashion designers, illustrators, teachers. Edited and augmented by Emma von Sichart. Translated by Alexander K. Dallas. 594 illustrations. 464pp. 5⅛ x 7⅛.

21030-8 Paperbound $3.00

CHINESE HOUSEHOLD FURNITURE, G. N. Kates. A summary of virtually everything that is known about authentic Chinese furniture before it was contaminated by the influence of the West. The text covers history of styles, materials used, principles of design and craftsmanship, and furniture arrangement—all fully illustrated. xiii + 190pp. 5⅝ x 8½.

20958-X Paperbound $1.75

THE COMPLETE WOODCUTS OF ALBRECHT DURER, edited by Dr. Willi Kurth. Albrecht Dürer was a master in various media, but it was in woodcut design that his creative genius reached its highest expression. Here are all of his extant woodcuts, a collection of over 300 great works, many of which are not available elsewhere. An indispensable work for the art historian and critic and all art lovers. 346 plates. Index. 285pp. 8½ x 12¼.

21097-9 Paperbound $3.00

Dover publishes books on commercial art, art history, crafts, design, art classics; also books on music, literature, science, mathematics, puzzles and entertainments, chess, engineering, biology, philosophy, psychology, languages, history, and other fields. For free circulars write to Dept. DA, Dover Publications, Inc., 180 Varick St., New York, N.Y. 10014.